忍者武士暗殺者

DEADLY VIPER
CHARACTER ASSASSINS

MIKE FOSTER & JUD WILHITE

侍

a kung fu survival guide for life & leadership.
proceed with caution.

暗 殺 者

ZONDERVAN

Deadly Viper Character Assassins
Copyright © 2007 by Mike Foster and Jud Wilhite

This title is also available as a Zondervan ebook. Visit www.zondervan.com/ebooks.

This title is also available in a Zondervan audio edition. Visit www.zondervan.fm.

Requests for information should be addressed to:
Zondervan, *Grand Rapids, Michigan 49530*

ISBN 978-0-310-29323-1

Visit DeadlyViper.org

Cover and interior design by Plain Joe Studios in Corona, CA
Author photo by Eric Cotter
Comic on pages 157 – 158 by Ghostlight Creative (Sal Garcia, Ray Sanchez, and Josh Webb).
www.ghostlightcreative.com

Printed in China

09 10 11 12 13 14 15 • 24 23 22 21 20 19 18 17 16 15 14 13 12 11 10 9 8 7 6 5 4 3 2 1

CONTENTS

Chapter 0

Nunchucks, & Warriors, & Master Po

HE WHO CONQUERS HIMSELF IS THE GREATEST WARRIOR.
—MASTER PO, *KUNG FU*

Kung fu and hard knocks drove us to this place.

Maybe you're here with us. Not physically, of course. Just at this place in life.

We write this from Jud's Man Cave. Rest assured this is no bunker filled with raw meat and rifles. It's just a converted part of Jud's garage with a couple of leather chairs, a TV, and some good action movies.

Not long ago, we were in the Man Cave watching the *Kung Fu* episode where Master Po says — gently, wisely — "He who conquers himself is the greatest warrior."

For some reason, we paused and just had this "moment." We put down our four-cheese, pepperoni, and sausage pizza slices simultaneously. Was it guilt? Was it a strange sense of our own mortality? Was it simply that we forgot the mushrooms?

The episode droned on though we weren't listening to it anymore. Mike took the opportunity to ask, "Hey Jud, how's it going? Really, how's it going?"

That kicked off the discussion that became this little guide. We talked over the stresses of our work, our marriages, our friendships, and life in general. We kicked around our options for the future. We talked about our dreams for our kids, and our roles as leaders. We hashed over the possible pitfalls of life. (Mike heads up a design firm; Jud's a pastor.) That night we got honest with each other and ourselves and asked some pretty straight up questions:

- How come we never talk about the really important stuff?
- What are those big and nasty issues lurking out there ready to take us down?
- What are those stupid choices we are on the verge of making that would deliver a knockout blow and wreck our lives?
- How could we help each other be healthier leaders and find true meaning for our lives?

And out of that conversation in the garage came this kung fu survival guide.

快 LADIES AND GENTLEMEN, WE INTRODUCE YOUR ENEMIES

We will be introducing you to seven mortal enemies, the assassination squad. We refer to them as the Deadly Viper Character Assassins. Who are these kung fu killers? They are bloodthirsty hit-men lurking in the shadows plotting to undermine your leadership, integrity, and success. And

Jud Takes Out a Black Belt (sort of)

Once Jud knocked out a black belt in Karate with a pair of nunchucks. As a young teenager he was showing off a cool move over his right arm when he adjusted just a little too much and accidentally nailed his friend in the back of the head. He collapsed on the floor, out cold. Thankfully, he came to and Jud apologized profusely. But you gotta admit, knocking out a because of their stealth MO, we often don't see them untill it's too late. By then, they're chopping us up into sushi rolls and folding us into puny cream cheese wontons.

The Deadly Vipers are some bad dudes who take great pleasure in what they do. They eat your kind for lunch and are skilled in the arts of annihilation, pain, and destruction. These ninja experts are working twenty-five hours a day, eight days a week to undo you. They don't rest. These forces of darkness are fully funded and well resourced. They possess the weapons, they've plotted the strategies, and they kick more tail before 7:00 a.m. than most of us will our entire lives.

And then there's little old us looking like schoolgirls with plaid skirts on because we are unskilled and undisciplined in the area of character. We're weaklings with rail-skinny arms and toothpick legs. Too many of us think we can skate by on our business savvy, stellar successes, and our impressive ability to jive talk ourselves out of anything. But here's the deal: the Deadly Vipers aren't in the mood for small talk. They're in the mood for spilling blood. They're like our favorite karate legend, Chuck Norris; the Deadly Vipers don't go hunting, they go a killing.

Our goal with this guide is to help you be ready to face these brutal slayers. We want to turn you into warriors who are trained and ready for wherever the attacks may come from. And let's make this one truth crystal clear: the Character Assassins are on their way. For some of you they are pressing a steely blade to your throat even now.

南 UGLY DANCE PARTNERS

Here is a fundamental problem as we see it: character and integrity are like those girls or guys at the high school dance you would only cut the rug with as a last resort. It's as if they are sitting across the dance hall wearing headgear, braces, and Coke bottle glasses. Want to dance? No thanks! As our friend, Brad, who puts on huge conferences for next-generation leaders, said, "If we did a conference on character and integrity, no one would come."

For too long the discussions on character have been marginalized by politically correct business jargon, legalistic strategies from do-gooders, and concepts that only fire up sixty-something IBM execs.

Deep down we know we need to keep the issues of character and integrity, and the ongoing options to screw them up, before us. But everyone's short on time, running fast, and has nanosecond attention spans. We (we being Mike and Jud) also realize it's critical to talk about these things in ways everyone can understand. So we kept this book short, used a lot of pictures, and wrote a survival guide you can get through on a flight from LA to New York. We will honor you fellow warriors by utilizing speed and velocity for the download and for the next steps.

Deadly Viper Character Assassins is a simple book on character for the rest of us. No psychobabble, no research-driven clinical discussion. We are not Peter Drucker, Stephen Covey, or rocket scientists. We aren't gurus on anything and have much to learn ourselves. We're just two guys who have begun a strategic conversation with each other on the topic of integrity. We now invite you, our fellow Grasshoppers, to join us.

Deadly Viper is no-holds barred. It's for the radical, risk-taking, gutsy leaders who are kicking butt and taking names. Even if you're in the middle of your finest hour, basking in a pool of success, we sense there might be some personal integrity stuff you need to think about. It's very possible your character weapons have dulled and your integrity muscles have become flabby and soft. And you haven't even noticed.

Without doubt some of you are stuck, right now, in a pretty ugly situation. You've been sliced and diced by a character assassin and you've made some deadly miscalculations. Maybe you've been publicly humiliated and branded a cheat, a liar, and a first-class loser. Perhaps your fair-weather friends have stopped calling in your time of need and you feel the eyes of condemnation on you. As wounded leaders you may believe the only job you'll ever get in the future will be at your local McDonald's managing how many chocolate sprinkles to shake onto a customer's McFlurry.

You see, fellow Grasshopper, this book is also for those of us who ran fast and hard and screwed things up – or at least smacked the guardrails pretty hard. We care a lot more about the banged up and bruised than the pretty and perfect. We're two guys who are cheering for those who have spectacularly smashed up their life and leadership reputations.

乐 NO PERFECT PEOPLE

Many think being a person of integrity is about perfectionism, legalism, and the glow of a halo illuminating your face. Please don't make us hurl. Unfortunately, the issue of character has often been hijacked by behavior Nazis who wield their nattering lists of do's and don'ts. We will have none of that here. We would rather bring the decades-old wisdom of the great Eagles musician, Glenn Frey, to the table: "Rock and roll isn't about perfection. It's about excellence."

So is integrity. No one passes through life's rich pageant without character flaws. No one bats .1000 in integrity, either. See, whether it's big or little stuff, we all got stuff. Maybe we
- under-report our taxes,
- exaggerate successes,
- say things we don't mean,
- carry on an illicit affair, or
- take advantage of people.

WARNING!

This product is sold for use in **HIGH RISK** activities. Consult

your physician prior to starting any training program.

Injuries, including **PARALYSIS** and **DEATH,**

can occur when using this product.

USER ASSUMES ALL RISK OF INJURY!

MADE IN CHINA.*

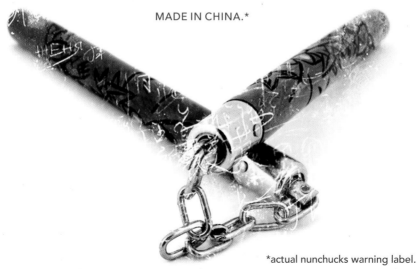

*actual nunchucks warning label.

Or maybe we
- ➤ steal pens and paper from the office,
- ➤ surf porn during work hours,
- ➤ enjoy gossiping and undermining people,
- ➤ rip our kids off with the lack of quality time, or
- ➤ bail on friends in their time of need.

Bottom line: We're all a mess, and we all have character issues.

明 THE DESTINATION WILL COME. THE JOURNEY IS NOW.

Ralph Waldo Emerson wrote, "The force of character is cumulative." We need leaders to slip into a rhythm of making right choices. Imagine character just naturally flowing from you because you have trained and disciplined your mind, body, and soul. Choosing honor, nobility, and the good can become extensions of who we are. We reject the small-minded, ineffective approach of those who focus simply on specific bad behaviors and miss the lifestyle approach. All of us want to get to the point where living with integrity is as simple as clubbing baby seals over the melon. (BTW, we love baby seals so don't miss our point.)

You can get good at this if you want to, but ultimately it's your choice. It will come with a cost, and there will be sacrifice. You can treat this like all those other "nice thoughts" or "leadership concepts" you've heard from well-meaning folks, or you can train your mind, body, and soul to flow with integrity.

来 MISTAKES, GRACE, MORE MISTAKES, GREATER GRACE

Let's start here: life is about mistakes, grace, more mistakes, and then greater grace. Character isn't a destination, but a journey toward becoming a more whole, complete, and healthy leader.

If you think you've got it all together, please put this book down immediately, dial 1-800-IMSOGREAT, wait for the beep, and tell the lovely operator standing by how you figured out all you've figured out. In your case, this little guide will be an utter waste of your time. But if you

- are looking to be a better leader, friend, or person
- want to learn a couple things about the pitfalls of life
- have messed up and aren't sure where to go from here

we have some good news, some sweet tips, and a few insights on how we can grab hold of sustained meaning for our lives.

盟 RADICAL GRACE AND RADICAL INTEGRITY

We believe in radical grace as much as we do radical integrity. A true warrior lives in both "Zen-like" states. So let us be blunt with you: if you don't give grace or mercy to the defeated, you are not a noble leader. Consider the end of a great kung fu movie where the hero has conquered his opponent and we eagerly await the fatal martial arts blow. It's time for the chop-chop of the loser's head.

忍者武士暗殺者

But the hero doesn't do it. He restrains himself. Why? True warriors live above vengeance and judgment and embrace the principles of mercy and grace.

A society that takes pleasure in the failures of others lacks honor and dignity. Unfortunately, every day we indulge our fix for gossip and scandal by buying the tabloid rags that tell tales of a pastor's gay sex scandal, a celebrity's mental breakdown, or a politician being caught in bed with a fifty-dollar hooker and a crack pipe. We are a putrid people if we enjoy this sludge and are entertained by the downfall of our fellow person. It is not the way of the warrior. It lacks beauty, honor, and strength.

乐 NO LONE RANGERS

It's also important to understand this book isn't just about you and your deal. Character is both a personal AND a community concept. If you are a person of great character, all those around you benefit. The organization, the relationships, the families—they all win. If you lack character, everyone pays.

The building of character is a community thing. There are no Lone Rangers. We need to train together, fight together, and watch each other's backs. True leaders make tough decisions to battle for integrity together no matter how inconvenient or how it may stretch us.

Most of us are simply not inclined to talk about our struggles, our inadequacies, and our vulnerabilities with each other. This is counter

culture. But we must. We must defend each other in this battle and carry each other's burdens. If Jud was ever to be peering at the tip of a saber belonging to a character assassin, without question Mike would fiercely battle for his friend. If Mike was in a potentially deadly place, Jud would do the same. We are linked together, each and every one of us.

If you are not willing to defend and come to the aid of a wounded, struggling – even fallen leader – then your character is vacant and empty. If you lack the guts to risk your personal reputation for someone else, then Master Po rejects you. And yes, we are dead serious. In fact, we're not sure there is anything more cowardly, more anti-warrior, less noble than attacking an obviously bruised leader – or standing on the sidelines, silently and smugly taking in the spectacle of it all.

明 THE GRAND MASTER CHALLENGE

Our basic conclusion is that we need to make character and integrity THE priority. We need to train, get ripped, and be ready for the fight. You want to rock the world, Grasshopper? Then make these issues the foundation for life. So we are asking you to make a choice and a decision right now. We are asking you to go balls out with us and become warriors, fighters, and black belts in the art of integrity. For some, this might be painful. For others, this will simply validate your leadership choices and good decisions.

This is the grand master challenge to conquer yourself. We want to party with Master Po! We are warriors in the making.

Chapter 1

The Assassin of Character Creep

> THE CEO WHO MISLEADS OTHERS IN PUBLIC
> WILL EVENTUALLY MISLEAD HIMSELF IN PRIVATE.
> – WARREN BUFFETT

There is a classic form of martial arts that doesn't usually make it into the movies, but is greatly feared among martial artists. It stems from Thailand and utilizes and maximizes the short stature and native speed of the Thai people.

It's all about short, quick strikes to the opponent's knees and below. There are no real haymakers in this system or impressive body blows. Just precise, very effective thrusts that take out a ligament here, bruise a nerve there, hyperextend an arch, and finally compromise your footing. They don't go for your head, or major organs; they focus their deadly clips on a small yet critical part of your body. These karate experts viciously nibble away at your legs until you are completely incapacitated and collapse in defeat.

It's also very much like the way small compromises in integrity and character can take out your leadership footing and lead to death at the hands of the Assassin of Character Creep.

加 CREEP

Nobody wakes up and decides to tank their lives and careers because of integrity issues. We don't make an entry in our diary one day: "Dear Diary, today I plan to commit fraud which will eventually lead to the demise of my career, a nervous breakdown, and ultimately jail." Character Creep happens subtly and slowly. It is a methodical process where small compromises and rationalizations lead to areas we never thought we would go. We drew lines in the sand and then subtly erased them.

Jim Collins writes of those whose careers went down with the fiascoes at Enron, Worldcom, and others:

> These were people who, in the presence of an opportunity to behave differently, got drawn into it, one step after another. If you told them ten years ahead of time, "Hey, let's cook the books and all get rich," they would never go along with it. But that's rarely how most people get drawn into activities that they later regret.[1]

Character Creep slowly steals integrity. One expense account gets falsely padded, but it's not really a big deal. We "borrow" a little here and a little there. Maybe we even tell ourselves we plan to pay it back. We keep rationalizing and justifying and pretty soon, we find ourselves in a tangled web of financial impropriety.

Moment by moment we are building a life, a reputation. Too often we don't realize the compounding effect of those moments. Tennessee Titans football star Pacman Jones got his wakeup call when the NFL Commissioner suspended him for the entire 2007 football season. After

忍者武士暗殺者

being interviewed by police on ten different occasions, the final straw occurred in Vegas after a shooting at a strip club.

Pacman's choices hurt his future, his family, his team, and his wallet. He'll lose $1,292,500 in base pay. In response to the suspension, Pacman offered an apology in a full page ad in *USA Today*. It began: "At age twenty-three, I never thought my life would come to a crossroads."

We never think it will happen to us – until it does.

We've known too many people who are brighter, more talented, and more grounded than us who succumbed to Character Creep and didn't even realize how their lives were being impacted. Eventually the Chinese proverb became true of them: "He has too many lice to feel an itch."

年 WHAT'S AT STAKE?

Why should we care? Because there is too much at stake to play games.

- ➤ Our families are at stake.
- ➤ Our careers are at stake.
- ➤ Our impact in the world is at stake.

Everything we have worked so hard to build can be destroyed in a matter of moments. And yes, in fact, we are trying to freak you out. How many CEOs do we have to read or hear about in the news? How many political

CHARACTER CREEP

WE'VE KNOWN TOO MANY PEOPLE WHO ARE BRIGHTER, MORE GROUNDED, AND MORE TALENTED THAN US WHO SUCCUMBED TO "CHARACTER CREEP" AND DIDN'T EVEN REALIZE HOW THEIR LIVES WERE BEING IMPACTED.

WE MUST REALIZE
THAT LIFE IS ABOUT
THE RIVETS,
the little details.

and religious leaders, and culturally influential artists, entertainers, and athletes must fall before we start to take this stuff seriously? And those are just the ones we hear about. Countless individuals lose their jobs, families, even their freedom, because of the handiwork of the silent assassin that is Character Creep.

盟 RIVETS

In July of 2007, we were on a trip in Ecuador with Wess Stafford, the president of Compassion International. He shared with us some thoughts on leadership and talked of what really sank the Titanic on April 15, 1912. Most people think an iceberg sank the ship, but that is only half the story. Many similar ships had collided with icebergs and emerged intact. And it would have been virtually impossible for an iceberg to penetrate the double thick steel hull of the Titanic. No, the Titanic sank because of three million faulty rivets that held the steel to the ship's hull. Apparently, during the manufacturing of these rivets, the plant cut a few corners and used sub-standard iron to save a few bucks. The force of the collision with the iceberg created immense pressure on the rivets, which caused them to catastrophically fail. Thus, the steel plating of the ship's hull catapulted off the frame allowing the freezing waters of the Atlantic to rush inside the doomed ship.

We must realize life is about the rivets, the little details. We must acknowledge whether we are cutting corners and identify where we are vulnerable. When the pressure comes, will we be able to stand the force, or will our hull be compromised?

明 **TRUE FRIENDS STAB YOU IN THE FRONT**

As two people committed to a meaningful life, we regularly challenge the little things in each other's lives. We find a faulty rivet, we call it out. We don't hold back. From the tone of voice we use with associates, to our negative attitudes, to the neglect of our physical and spiritual health, we don't hesitate to call it out.

If you're not willing to be bold with fellow friends to the point of risking the friendship, then your friendship has superficial value. Oscar Wilde once said, "True friends stab you in the front."

At times it's brutally blunt and we have to say things that are going to cut us. But if we don't say it, few people in our lives will. And here is a well-known fact: the more senior your leadership role is, the less honest criticism you'll receive from those around you. If you are responsible for someone's paycheck then consider their "honest" opinion of you only partially true. They are holding back what they really want to say because calling your boss on the carpet for his lack of character is usually not a stellar career move.

The nice thing about our friendship is we are not connected in a professional context. Jud doesn't determine Mike's pay raises at the design studio, and Mike doesn't do Jud's performance review at the church. This provides for a lot of freedom in our conversations and cultivates a "let it fly" posture with absolutely no hindrances. Mike can tell Jud without any reservations,

忍者武士暗殺者

"You're being a complete jerk to your wife right now. Stop it and go apologize." And that goes both ways.

When we both lived closer to one another, we'd meet every Thursday at a Denny's. We adopted a little slogan after reading about a minister in California who was pictured in a hot tub with a topless woman who was married to another man:

> **Keep your pants up, keep your hands off the money, and keep your butt out of the hot tub.**

It was our mantra. We also discussed our theory of "success by default." You see, you don't have to be the most gifted leader or person. If you just stay faithful over the long haul, carefully manage the small things, then you'll be the last person standing! You will have attained success by default.

民 SECOND CHANCE BUSINESS

Now, suppose you've taken the kind of dive we're talking about. You're not finished. Just because you fudge or erase the lines doesn't mean you can't redraw them. You can always go back and reclaim lost ground.

Recently we had the opportunity to hang out with Duane Chapman (a.k.a. "Dog the Bounty Hunter") and his wonderful wife, Beth, for a couple days. (Mike still refuses to wash the cheek that Beth kissed him on.) They're a lot of fun, but they've been through a lot. Dog grew up in one of the toughest

忍者武士暗殺者

sections of Denver. He learned to defend himself early on. Eventually, Dog fell in with a motorcycle gang. As sergeant of arms for "The Devil's Disciples," he got into, well, trouble.

Dog was arrested eighteen times for armed robbery. He ended up spending time in prison for murder one, not as the triggerman but for simply being present at a drug related shooting. (In Texas, at the time, that made Dog as guilty as the guy who pulled the trigger.)

That event marked a point of change for Dog. "As I was entering prison, I made up my mind I was going to change back into something that my mother planned. I changed my life at that second, even though I did eighteen months behind bars after that."

Dog owed two hundred dollars a month in child support when he got out of prison. He couldn't find a job because of his criminal record. The judge had heard that Dog had run down an inmate while he was in prison. So the judge said to him, "I have this guy who ran away. He's wanted for sexually assaulting a child. Can you go and get him? And I'll pay you."

Dog was happy to oblige the judge. "Sure, I'll go get the guy!" Soon the judge tossed him the names of six other guys to capture. Eventually he referred Dog to a bail bondsman, and the rest is TV history.

We are saying there is an inefficiency in the market place because the market place doesn't properly value this characteristic of character. And all we're doing is taking advantage of that mispricing in the market and trying to make money off of it. We don't approach our investment from a moralistic standpoint, but we believe that the world and the market place doesn't fully understand the value of character. Really at the heart of it is that being good wins.

- Dan Cooper
from Fox River Financial describing their strategy of investing into companies where the integrity of the CEO is strategically valued.

Dog has now been a bounty hunter for almost twenty-seven years. He's caught more than six thousand people. His reality show on *A&E* is the most watched show on the network. Some even say Dog the Bounty Hunter is the biggest reality TV star in the world.

All that's truly impressive. Yet the core message of Dog's life is even more impressive:

You can start over, no matter what happens.

Dog challenges many of the people he nabs to rebuild their lives. He says, "We are second chance people in the second chance business." He should know. He's a living example.

家 BE READY FOR THE CREEP

Today, you can come clean and acknowledge where the Assassin of Character Creep has moved into your world. You can seek to redraw the lines and make things right before more damage is done. And you can be assured that this Creep is waiting to strike you again. How can you prepare for his next attack?

First, re-evaluate the smallest areas of your life and business practice. This is where the Creep strikes first. We recently sat down with Marcus Buckingham, the bestselling author of *Now, Discover Your Strengths* and *The One Thing You Need To Know*. Marcus is an elite business sage who has Fortune 500 companies busting down his door for consulting services. But when he chatted with us about the issues of character, it was clear Marcus demanded integrity in the smallest of things.

He said, "If someone wants to talk to me and I'm in the office and I don't want to talk to them, my assistant doesn't say, 'He's on the phone,' when really I'm not on the phone. She can say, 'He's unavailable,' but she can't say, 'He is on the phone.' She can't say, 'He stepped out for a minute and he is not in the office.' Those are very small examples, but with me and my company you don't say something that isn't true. You don't necessarily volunteer all of the information like, 'Right now he is cleaning his toenails and he can't talk to you.' You don't have to do that, but you can't lie."

He shared another example with us of how he prevents character creep. "If we do a speech through a speaking bureau, the ethics of the business is such that if that client wants to do another speech, you book it again through the speaking bureau. Though many times the client will call us up directly, we deliberately send them back to the bureau so they can book it and take their percentage. Now technically we wouldn't have to do that. Nobody would know anyway, but it's part of our ethic. It's what we do. So whenever there are opportunities to take shortcuts, we don't."

It is clear that Marcus has examined the details of his life and business. He's worked hard to ensure integrity takes place in the smallest of details.

THE FUTURE

BELONGS TO THOSE WHO PREPARE FOR IT.

– ralph waldo emerson

What are the seemingly unimportant decisions in your life? Are you managing them with integrity? They really do matter. The simple defense against Character Creep is to pay attention to the little adjustments. That's because the little adjustments, both positive and negative, become huge over a long period of time. A quick example: John, who was a good friend of ours, decided one day to stop wearing his wedding ring because it was "uncomfortable" and was bothering his finger. Mike suggested to John that he should get a tattoo on his ring finger that looked like a wedding band. John wasn't interested in Mike's lame idea and he continued to not wear his ring. Guess what? Six months after this conversation, our buddy John had an affair with a coworker and tanked his marriage. Though it's a small piece of jewelry and a seemingly insignificant choice – whether or not to wear a ring – it shouts to all potential hoochie-mamas and Don Juans that we are back on the market.

Another way we defend against this assassin is to live by a basic mode of operation: refrain from doing anything today we'd be uncomfortable reading about in the headlines tomorrow, watching on the eleven o'clock news, or being broadcast to thousands of people.

Mike experienced this axiom first hand. Back in 2003, I (Mike) had an independent documentary film crew following me around for a few years as I went about my work and mission. At the time, a venture I'd started called XXXchurch.com, which was designed to help people struggling with porn addiction, had attracted lots of media attention. I had cameras recording my actions and microphones picking up every word. After a while, I would often forget the cameras were even there. They became almost invisible. This was great for the filmmaker but not so great for me.

When I saw the final film called *Missionary Positions*, I must confess there were a few scenes that caused me to cringe because of my actions. As I sat there in the theater with friends, family, and strangers, I squirmed, sweated, and couldn't bear to watch as my questionable judgment and behavior was broadcast onto a thirty-foot wide movie screen. I was especially embarrassed at the scene where I mocked and made fun of little people (that's the preferred term used by people who for biological reasons don't conform to standard growth rates). I basically made a huge joke about somebody's disability. I couldn't believe I did that, but there it was in full cinematic color. Seeing how my actions yesterday were being broadcast today, brought a lot of clarity into my life.

How would your life change if you knew you'd see it all played out on television tomorrow? We challenge you to live each day as if those details could be broadcast to the world. Living this way provides a fatal blow to this assassin.

Recognize this: the Assassin of Character Creep is out there waiting for you to bend the truth, mismanage small decisions, and take a haphazard approach to the details. It's time to find some sand and draw a line.

DUANE CHAPMAN

a.k.a. dog the bounty hunter

Stars in Dog the Bounty Hunter, one of the most watched reality TV shows on television.

Has made more than six thousand captures in twenty-seven years of bounty hunting.

Dog, what is most important to you in life now?

To me, as I get older, the most important thing in life is death. What comes after life? What is important to me is to leave a good legacy for my children. For them to think, "Dog was a good dude." Also, to have a connection with God.

What helps you maintain your character?

It is a lot easier living with integrity than living as I once did and having to wonder, "Did I leave a finger print? Was there a camera?" So what keeps me on the straight and narrow is that it could go immediately, your fifteen minutes of fame could become your fifteen minutes of shame. People won't listen to you anymore. Right now in my life, when Dog speaks, people listen. It's kind of like that whole E.F. Hutton thing. If people ain't listening, you're done. That's what holds me together, knowing the other side. I don't want that.

TO HEAR MORE, VISIT DEADLYVIPER.ORG

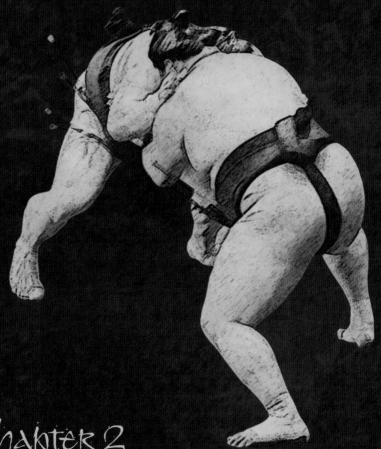

Chapter 2

the assassin of zi qi qi ren

IF YOU TELL THE TRUTH,
YOU DON'T HAVE TO REMEMBER ANYTHING.
– MARK TWAIN

There is a killer called Zi Qi Qi Ren. No, this is not some communicable disease, but it certainly is deadly. This funky Chinese word literally means "self-deception while deceiving others." When Mao Zedong ruled China, it was a time of telling fantasies to yourself and others about what was truly happening. Zi Qi Qi Ren gripped the nation.

Self-deception reached its peak in the country. Poor Chinese peasants would move their crops from several plots of land down to just one plot of land to demonstrate to government Party officials and visitors that they had produced a so-called "miracle harvest." The "miracle" field would be filled with all kinds of fruits and vegetables, and that would impress everyone who saw it.

However, it wasn't an accurate portrait of the farm's productivity. They manipulated the results. The visitors and Party officials would leave, the transplanted crops would die, and these villagers were left starving. But surprisingly, these peasants continued this practice over and over again. Even though this deception was killing them and causing them to starve, they continued on with the lethal charade. They misled Party officials, visitors, and most importantly they deceived themselves.

Zi Qi Qi Ren is alive and well in leaders today. Consider Miss USA winner Tara Conner, who epitomized beauty and American values. She said the right things, smiled perfectly, helped worthy causes, and yet her life was secretly spinning out of control.

Our pride, and our unwillingness to acknowledge that we are human beings with frailties, leads us to conceal. Too many of us employ fake personas and play multiple roles. We are pretending to be good employees and friends. When you pretend, there is nothing "good" about that.

年 WHY ARE YOU LYING?

Somewhere along this road we have concluded that in order to be liked by others we need to hide our true self. Early on we learned that in order to be accepted in society we had to be well adept in the art of "shuck and jive." As children growing up we learned to chew with our mouths closed, not to write with pen on the walls, and of course how to lie with the best of them.

From the beginning of recorded history, humans have been covering mistakes and embarrassments. We once hid our goof-ups with large fig leaves placed in strategic locations. Now we cover ourselves with half-truths, shameless puffery, and exaggerations. We hide our junk, weaknesses, and frailties in a very large closet in our soul.

Master Kan of *Kung Fu* fame spoke,

To suppress a truth is to give it force beyond endurance.

联 OUR LITTLE FAKE SELVES

Some of the most tragic stories we know involve those who tried so desperately to be something they are not.

Jason, who lives near Mike in Southern California, is owner and founder of a two hundred million dollar company. He flies around in a fancy private jet. Jason has a sweet mansion overlooking the Pacific Ocean and from outward appearances is an absolute success.

But what most people don't know is that he is a broken man whose destructive sex addiction is eating him alive. Jason's addiction has cost him several marriages. He has a rocky relationship with his kids on good days. He feels completely helpless and out of control.

However, he hides this fact really, really well. You'd never suspect that his life is this way. If you met Jason, you would want to be just like him.

WE HIDE ALL OUR

JUNK, WEAKNESSES, AND FRAILTIES

IN A VERY LARGE CLOSET IN OUR SOUL.

it's time to **stop hiding.**

When was the last time you had a completely honest conversation with someone that you trust?

So let's ask a few tough questions:

- What areas of my life am I most prone to be deceptive about? (If you say you don't have any such areas, you've just identified one.)
- Why do I feel pressured to lie to certain people?
- Why do I think I need to lie?
- What'll happen when I'm found out?
- What would it feel like to stop lying and be free to be honest and open?

乐 NO MORE PRETENDING

You have one life, one role, and that is to be yourself. If you try to snow job your way through life, the Assassin of Zi Qi Qi Ren will carve your head off and cram it down your throat. Sure, there are private things in life. There are absolutely those things where, in a press conference, it is entirely legitimate to respond, "None of your business." But those things are few and far between.

Abraham Lincoln was once accused of being two-faced on a political issue. He offered this classic response:

> If I had another face, do you think I'd wear this one?

When we conceal, we give this Deadly Viper an all-access pass to wreak havoc in our lives, careers, families, and relationships. If you want to experience self-respect and true liberation in life, take responsibility for the *whole* package.

姐 FROM CONCEALMENT TO TRANSPARENCY

One of the practical things we do to be transparent is that we have a program on our computers that tracks all the websites we go to. It then shoots out a report every two weeks to our friends showing the sites that we visited. It is just a simple way to open our lives to each other. We also know each other's passwords and codes to each other's computers and email accounts. Again, we've earned the right to have this access with each other, and we know we can trust each other with this information.

Concealment can happen in a variety of forms and for various reasons. Secrets seem to make everything better until they make everything worse. That's right: with every situation we try to cover up, the truth eventually comes out. The rooster *will* eventually come home to roost, and he *is* going to have his way with those hens.

Our friend, Craig Groeschel, has been married seventeen years and leads a large church. When we talked with him about pursuing transparency in his life he said, "Every leader must answer this question: What is the one thing you're afraid of? Then go talk about it immediately. Bring it into the light. I know I'm the type of person who could fall into a dark place, but what keeps me strong is that I tell people immediately." He tells them everything and is brutally honest and confessional. He describes it as getting emotionally "naked" before them. It is key for his health as a leader and for the organization.

Craig also suggests that we should have two levels of transparency. The first level is to find people you can be fully transparent with. But then he suggests there's a second group of people you are almost transparent with and tell most things, but not everything. Inviting trusted people into your life is a great way to combat concealment.

Craig says, "We also do our best to systematically reward confession. We are deliberately creating a 'confession culture' with our staff. If you confess it, then we can help you. If you hide it and we find out, then there are serious consequences."

临 PRECEDENT OF GRACE

Writer Anne Lamott says much of our life is spent doing the crazy mental arithmetic of how, at any given moment, we might improve (or at least disguise) our screw-ups in more charming ways. She goes on to say that human beings want and need the same things: to belong, feel safe, and to be respected.

A new model of belonging, respect, and grace is needed to move from a culture of concealment at work to a culture of honesty. We must hold high the values of forgiveness and second chances.

WHAT ARE YOUR SECRETS THAT YOU

ARE AFRAID MIGHT COME OUT? IS IT BETTER

TO LIVE IN

FEAR OR FREEDOM?

We can make a difference by leading out of our own personal weaknesses, and in so doing change this toxic culture of perfectionism and image management. We've all worshiped at this altar far too long. We have transferred perfectionism into our work culture and with those who work with us. Too often we create scenarios and environments that lack compassion, and thus we send ourselves and those around us into hiding.

Why would anyone be honest if they knew they were going to risk losing their job, relationships, and endure embarrassment or shame as a result? Unfortunately, we've worked with many organizations where only a masochist would be open with their failures. Admitting imperfection would result in being ground up, beaten down, and kicked to the curb. It's not right and it only perpetuates concealment. But we're Zi Qi Qi Ren junkies, anyway.

Psychologist Henry Cloud writes of an incident that happened when a young "superstar" CEO was given an opportunity to receive feedback from a more senior CEO.

> One of the more experienced guys looked up and said, "Want some feedback?" He said it in a way that left you wondering whether he was going to give sage advice or rail at the young man for being out to lunch in some way. There was just no way to tell from his poker face. But I will never forget the young superstar's immediate response: "By all means. Give me a gift."

He saw the feedback, whatever it was, as a gift because it could give him some reality that he did not know. I remember thinking, "We will be watching this guy's accomplishments for a long time."[2]

You see, honesty is a gift. Whether in meetings, our own lives, or in welcoming feedback, truth brings freedom and is life giving. We have this saying, popularized by Alcoholics Anonymous, that we often share with each other that we are only as sick as our secrets. The only way for a secret or a weakness to have power over us is to hold it in.

I (Mike) remember a late night phone call where I confessed to Jud about this volatile situation I found myself in. I was in Chicago on business and was being picked up for a forty-five minute ride to a speaking engagement. As the Lincoln Town Car pulled up, an extremely attractive twenty-something woman popped out and said, "Hi Mike, I'm your driver." She was energetic, flirtatious, and I'd taken note. I climbed into the car and we started driving, just the two of us. Did I mention she was really attractive? Oh yeah, I did mention that.

We were hitting it off, really connecting, and I knew I had just crossed into a major danger zone. She was hot, and I was far from home where no one would ever know. I caught myself thinking thoughts I wouldn't want to see on a billboard anytime soon; I realized how easily things could happen that

I'd later regret. I knew I had to shut this whole thing down. So I did. But, I was so embarrassed by my stupid actions and idiotic behavior.

Then of course, I had a choice after this whole thing went down. I could either talk about it or I could conceal it.

It was hard to tell Jud this and it didn't come out quickly, but I'm glad I told him. We both shared some of our struggles in this area and made an agreement that night on the phone to never travel alone. We give ourselves two options now.

Option #1: We travel with a buddy or family member.

Option #2: If we don't travel with someone, we then stay at the homes of friends who live in the cities we're visiting.

Sure, it may cost us a couple hundred bucks for an extra airfare but it's totally worth it. And yes, we give up the nicely appointed Sheraton Hotel room with ESPN and FOXNEWS. In exchange we get to sleep in a room with Hello Kitty paraphernalia everywhere and bed down with Seymour the pet boa constrictor. Though in our opinion, it is a small price to pay. These options may not be practical for you if your work requires you to travel regularly. The important thing is to come up with some options that will work for you and live by them.

民 SECRECY IS DYING

A recent *Wired* magazine cover story on radical transparency declared that secrecy is dying. In fact Clive Thompson, in his article, "The See-Through CEO," boldly suggests that trying to hide anything these days is a bad idea. Especially in the world of the Internet and bloggers trying to scoop stories. Consider this:

- Microsoft was busted for offering to pay individuals money to improve the company's Wikipedia entry.
- Diebold, the maker of the electronic voting machines, adamantly claimed they were safe and secure until a professor posted a YouTube video that showed exactly how to hack them.

Thompson says, "In a world where Eli Lilly's internal drug-development memos, Paris Hilton's phonecam images, Enron's emails, and even the governor of California's private conversations can be instantly forwarded across the planet, trying to hide something illicit – trying to hide anything, really – is an unwise gamble." Thompson goes on to say, "Transparency is a judo move."[3] We would have to agree. And we suspect Master Po would concur.

乐 NEXT STEPS

So if you find yourself digging into this hole of concealment, our first challenge is to stop digging. Find yourself a good friend, full of grace and love for you, and give them 100% access. Everyone who hopes to defeat this assassin must have someone who has full rights to your private world.

Our strong suggestion: Think of who this person could be, write their name down in this book, and make a vow to yourself – do it right next to their name – that you are out of the concealment game and are going to be accountable in every way. Set up a meeting with that person at Starbucks and you'll be off and running. And so will the Assassin of Zi Qi Qi Ren who'll be forced to find someone else to prey on.

You can suffer in secrecy for a long time. Or, you can start being the leader you were – and are – meant to be.

RABBI DAVID WOLPE

Rabbi of Sinai Temple in Los Angeles.

Taught for ten years at the University of Judaism in LA and the Jewish Theological Seminary in New York.

WHAT DO YOU THINK ABOUT CHARACTER BEING BOTH A PERSONAL AND COMMUNAL THING?

Nobody is so smart that the counsel of others isn't without benefit. This is true even if others might have less experience or know less. You really do have to listen. In the end it comes to a counsel against arrogance. There are all sorts of different forms of subtle arrogance. But they come down to the monstrousness of an ego that doesn't believe that anyone else knows better and that what you do must always be right because you do it. And those things will kill you. You really do have to watch yourself.

Elie Weisel was here as our scholar in residence last year speaking to high school students, and in his last shot to talk to them he said, "Live higher and think deeper." That is exactly it. You can't put it any better than that. Although we are going to falter with that all the time, to have that as a guiding principle for your life can help.

If you have deep relationships, it shifts the center of your gravity from work to relationship. It lets you know what ultimately matters. Tomorrow, if you were fired from your job, work would be gone in an instant, but the relationships endure. That is what is lasting.

SHARE WITH US YOUR OPINION ON THE BENEFITS OF HAVING CHARACTER.

We have this idea that character ought to be rewarded. So when someone stands up for the right thing, they are shocked then that they don't get rewarded for it. But in fact, character is supposed to be its own reward and you don't necessarily do the right thing because you have this view that ultimately you will be rewarded.

Think about *High Noon*. The guy rides off in the end having lost his town and his community. He still has his wife, but he's not rewarded for what he did. That is the whole point of the movie. People watch that movie admiring him, and think that if I act like that I will be admired too. In some ways we get the wrong message from it. This is precisely why people won't necessarily admire you for it. If you whistle blow in a corporation, people might hate you for it! Does that make it wrong or just unrewarded? Those things are different. We live in a society where rewards are so extravagant. In America the rewards are all out of proportion to any skill. So knowing that, it is very hard then to maintain your character knowing that you might not be rewarded for it.

TO HEAR MORE, VISIT DEADLYVIPER.ORG

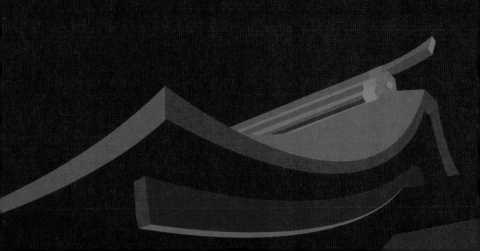

Chapter 3

THE ASSASSIN OF

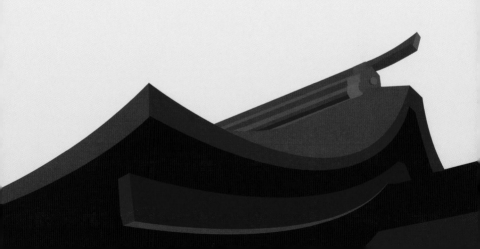

BECOME THE CALM AND RESTFUL BREEZE
THAT TAMES THE VIOLENT SEA.
– MASTER KAN, *KUNG FU*

Jud here. Awhile back, I began to struggle with extreme frustration and anger. I'd be impatient at home, curt and harsh with my kids, and pissed at the Dallas Cowboys football team. (Of course, Mike thinks this is entirely justified and easily fixed: just cheer for the San Diego Chargers.)

For a long time I blamed it on the fact that I was just too busy, too stressed, too overwhelmed. My excuses seemed justified, and I kept rationalizing this rage stewing inside.

One night my wife, Lori, was at the grocery store at our kids' bedtime so I had to put Emma and Ethan to bed. I was flying out for a big meeting the next morning, so I was in a rush and still needed to finish laundry and pack. Three different times my five-year-old daughter, Emma, climbed out of bed. Three different times I went upstairs and had to nag her to go to sleep. I grew more and more frustrated with the whole situation. Where's Lori? Why did she leave me in charge of the kids knowing I had so much to do tonight? While downstairs in the laundry room, I heard Emma's little feet hit the floor as she crawled out of bed for the fourth time.

I couldn't take it anymore and I just snapped. I went postal, psycho, and ballistic all at once. (Gifted and talented, wouldn't you say?)

My emotions cranked up and I was raging. I took it out by slamming my fist into the sheetrock of the Wilhite laundry room and leaving a hole in the wall. As Mark Twain put it, "When angry, count to five; when very angry, swear." And when very, very angry, hit something.

I stood there and thought, "Great! That's embarrassing! Real mature, Jud. What's next? Who or what will you swing at next time?"

Then a far more scary thought scrolled through: Is *this* what you are becoming?

That thought had the effect of sobering me up and calming me down. I went upstairs and tucked my daughter into bed. Then I returned to the laundry room and gazed at my handiwork and thought, "Lori will never see it; and if she does, I'll tell her I bumped into the wall with the broom handle." Totally lame, of course, but I was a desperate man.

Soon after this event, Lori walked right into the laundry room and asked, "Jud, why is there a hole in the wall?"

The Assassin

of Amped Emotions

lurks in the mundane

moments of

everyday life

Everything in me wanted to lie. I looked Lori in the eye and said, "Because your husband... uh... sort of... like... hit the wall." She raised her eyebrows.

Then I said, "Promise me you won't tell anyone." (This gave an extra lift to Lori's eyebrows.)

Later that day I took some time to reflect.

- Why am I getting so angry?
- Am I in control of my emotions?
- Why have I been exploding more and more lately?

Though it would have been easy to blame crammed schedules or the stresses at work, I had to get honest with the fact that it was my fault. I'd left myself (and consequently others around me) vulnerable to the Assassin of Amped Emotions.

Here is wisdom worth considering from Harriet Lerner:

Anger is a signal, and one worth listening to.

际 **AMPED, EMOTIONAL JIHADISTS**
The Assassin of Amped Emotions lurks in mundane moments of everyday life. We all have countless opportunities to completely transcend our normal selves and operate out of really unhealthy emotional places. We can instantly

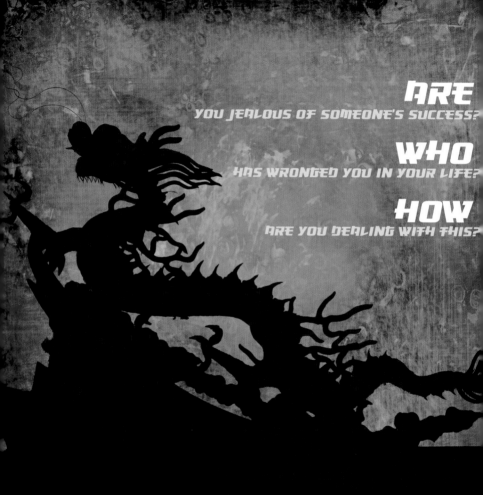

ARE
YOU JEALOUS OF SOMEONE'S SUCCESS?

WHO
HAS WRONGED YOU IN YOUR LIFE?

HOW
ARE YOU DEALING WITH THIS?

become jihadists and make some extremely toxic leadership decisions. Amped emotions can seep into our soul and infect our decision-making, character, and how we engage with others.

Maybe bitterness or jealousy or resentment is consuming you. Anyone can get on an emotional overload and then lash out. At a moment's notice you turn to the dark side and become your own worst enemy.

Maybe we find ourselves firing off those brutal emails that are in ALL CAPS and use a lot of exclamation marks. You know the ones we're talking about:

DEAR FREAKIN' IDIOT!!!
WHAT WERE YOU THINKING!!???!! DO YOU HAVE A BRAIN!!??
I WILL NOT STAND FOR THIS!!! PUSH ME AGAIN, YOU SCUM-SUCKING PENCIL-NECKED GEEK, AND I WILL MAKE YOU PAY!!!!!

Let's face it. The Assassin of Amped Emotions takes pleasure in taking you down. Here are his tactics:

- He wants you going nuts on petty and insignificant things.
- He wants you to embarrass yourself in front of your friends, coworkers, family, and associates.
- He wants you to act out and go postal.

Your emotional outbursts have the power to do a hit job on your reputation and severely undermine your ability to gain and retain the respect of others. This assassin wants you to feel threatened, insecure, and to be overly focused on your shortcomings. When this happens, he controls you and the timing of your ultimate downfall.

津 HOUSTON, WE HAVE A PROBLEM

Take Lisa Nowak, the jilted NASA astronaut who drove eighteen hours in her car across state lines to confront her former boyfriend's current flame – IN A DIAPER! She was so amped up on revenge she wasn't going to let a little poo-poo slow her down.

Think about it. Here's this elite professional, who has demonstrated extreme military discipline in the past. She's driving like a bat out of hell, apparently seeking a lover's revenge while wearing astronaut Pampers. Her ratcheted-up emotions and passion for payback sank her career and her future. The Assassin of Amped Emotions transformed this gifted astronaut into a loony space cadet.

Most leaders probably won't find themselves in this particular astronaut's situation, but we could certainly have our own loony adventures. This assassin's calling card has far more serious consequences than being the punch line to late-night television jokes, or even criminal prosecution.

One interesting study shows that the angrier we become, the more certain we are about our judgments. When we are angry, we "know" we are right. And that's a huge potential leadership fault, considering how emotions can mess up our ability to think rationally.

Time to ask another tough question:

What is it like to be on the other end of me?[4]

One time I (Mike) got pummeled by this assassin at work when I found out some interns had lost a day's worth of critical recordings we had just taped for a client. I was fuming, knowing we couldn't get it back. The simple lack of attention and priority had led to this failure. Well, I let my emotions take the driver's seat and I lost control. This is no exaggeration; I actually made one of the male interns who was responsible break down in tears and start sobbing. I know, I'm a jerk, and I felt horrible afterwards. I asked for his forgiveness and tried to make it right, but I will never get that moment back.

京 IDENTIFY YOUR PATHWAY
We need to positively identify the trigger points of our emotions. We need to assess those explosive pathways that lead us from "cool and collected" to "hot and bothered" to "furious and fuming."

Perhaps one trigger is a lack of respect. "Don't diss me or make me look bad in front of my people." Maybe you find your thoughts are transfixed on revenge or reprisal for being stabbed in the back by a friend. Are you replaying a messed-up event where you were made to look like a fool, or someone took advantage of your kindness? Are you ticked off at someone else's success or jealous of a colleague's limelight? Perhaps your ex-spouse is making your life a living hell and you want vengeance!

You can identify a few paths that could lead to those dark places, can't you?

Our friend, Jeff Brazil, who is a consultant and Pulitzer Prize-winning journalist, shared with us something he does that helps him keep his emotions in check in heated meetings. He says, "If I go into a business meeting, and I know it's likely to be a hostile environment for whatever reason – the other person and I just don't see eye to eye, or the circumstances are just emotionally volatile, or there's just a lot at stake – I write on my yellow notepad in big black letters the phrase: Rule #6. The rule is not original, I read it somewhere, but Rule #6 says, 'Don't take yourself too seriously.' I will refer to that pad of paper often in the meeting and it helps me try to remain composed when things get revved up."

来 MAD ABOUT THE RIGHT THINGS

But let's make one thing clear before we go further: it isn't our intention to turn you into this soft, spineless wussy who never has any passion or

our lives begin to end the day
we become silent about the

things
that matter.

- Martin Luther King Jr.

emotion. We're not trying to morph you into an android or some milquetoast leader who is a pushover. In fact, we want you energized, pumped up, and excited to take life by the horns.

That being said, we need to funnel our emotions toward things that really matter. If we're truly going to rock the world, we need to stop wasting so much juice on stupid, trivial stuff. Some of us need to grow up and stop acting like junior high wieners and stop thinking everything is about us.

Great leaders need to be hot under the collar about things like injustice, poverty, and racism. Things that matter. We've traveled together to some of the poorest parts of the world and can get pretty intense about poverty, especially when we see injustice accompanied by ignorance. People should be emotionally moved to right wrongs in the world and to stand up for those being taken advantage of. Martin Luther King Jr., Dorothy Day, Bono, and America's founding fathers all had plenty of emotion running through their veins. They weren't perfect, but we could learn a lot from them about the proper expressions of emotion. Our desire both for you and ourselves is that we are becoming fully alive, and helping others to do likewise. We could all benefit from laughing more, crying more, and choosing to feel more joyful, more grateful, more fulfilled. And it is a choice.

年 WHAT SHOULD WE DO?

Here are some of the practical things we do daily to help manage this assassin's attack:

- We refrain from reading attacks on ourselves whether it be in blogs, forums, or letters.
- If we are getting frustrated or irritated in a meeting, we will immediately call for a Coca-Cola break.
- We have a phrase called "Be the Duck" that we verbally say to ourselves and others. Like water rolls off the back of a duck, we encourage each other to let mistakes, failures, or letdowns roll off our back. "Be the Duck!"
- When we are really ticked or irritated, we unapologetically go to a movie. It's usually a violent flick with lots of killing and dismemberment. Healthy escapism has a way of bringing you back off the ledge.
- We do not use email to handle relationally-sensitive subjects or issues. We do it on the phone or face to face. Tone of voice and inflection are critical when dealing with heated items. Email offers none of that.
- We remind ourselves that if we crush or destroy someone in the organization, they will cease to contribute to the organization.

姐 FAST TO FORGIVE

So what else can you do right now to give this deadly viper a good whipping?

We made a pact with each other to be people who are fast to forgive. So much of our emotional volatility comes from relationships gone wrong. In the last couple years, both of us have dealt with severe betrayal by trusted friends and partners. We were deceived and lied to by these individuals and their actions were reprehensible. We would love to go into specific details about these people and name names, home phone numbers, and the organizations they currently lead, but we won't go there. As fellow warriors, we hold each other accountable to stay on the high road.

So how did we respond? Even though poisoning their pets, launching a full-blown smear campaign on the web, and reporting them to the IRS all seemed like good ideas at the time, we decided on none of those options. The path we chose was forgiveness. And we didn't do it because we are swell guys or some pushovers. We did it for us, and for our families, friends, and those who work with us.

You see, when you don't forgive someone, you let them park in your life forever. These people are like parasites that can suck the life right out of you and allow bitterness to rot you out. If you let these people and their actions haunt your thoughts, emotions, and spirit, you allow them to continually damage not only you but those around you, too.

So what we did was drop them like a rock and move on. And we mean that literally. We had a rock dropping ceremony. We put the offender's name on a stone, we wrote or imagined everything that we felt about the situation on that rock, and then we hurled it over a cliff and completely let it go. Mike did it in the mountains recently; Jud did it in the desert.

And don't start whining to us that it's too hard or unfair. You may be protesting right now saying, "Mike and Jud, you don't understand what happened to me. I couldn't do that. You don't understand the depth of my pain." Maybe we don't, but let's cut to the chase. You make the choice right now. You hold all the power. Do you want to be free or do you want to be chained to this person for the rest of your life? When you forgive you are made stronger, tougher, and life has new meaning. We know it will be hard, but it will be worth it. Some of you need to go find a big rock right now. Others need to find several. And while you're at it, rain down a few on top of the Assassin of Amped Emotions.

CATHERINE ROHR

- Founder and Executive Director of the Prisoner Entrepreneurship Program.

- Teaches business and entrepreneurial skills to inmates in Texas State Prisons.

- Left a high power venture capitalist job to help give prisoners a second chance.

WHAT DO YOU THINK ABOUT TRANSPARENCY AND BEING REAL WITH OTHERS?

Prison is the most authentic and transparent place ever. They see right through me. I see right through them. They are great game detectors. They are not afraid to call me out on stuff. They are always holding me accountable. I invite it. I seek out rebuke. I dish it out but I also take it. They are willing to make themselves so vulnerable in a place where it is absolutely not cool to be vulnerable. It's not gangsta. This inspires me to be more transparent. If someone is doing something wrong they will bring them before the class. We ask them on the spot to make a commitment to doing right. All of this is only possible because of transparency and accountability. They have seen the rewards of accountability. It is beneficial to them. The truth is, we all fall short. It's just some of us haven't been caught.

SO WHAT DO YOU TEACH THE GUYS ABOUT LIVING WITH CHARACTER?

We have ten driving values at PEP. Fresh start outlook. Servant leader mentality. Love, innovation, and accountability. Integrity. Execution. Fun. Excellence and wise stewardship. And within this, one of the biggest things related to our integrity value, and one of the hardest things to teach, is delayed gratification. That's what I focus on trying to teach them. Why would we choose a cheap solution? We always want immediate gratification. If we discover this discipline of delayed gratification then we will live with greater character. If there's nothing to look forward to then what's the point, right? Selling drugs is about immediate gratification. Fast payoff. Fast money. Fast women. For many of these guys, walking in the cap and gown at graduation is the first time they haven't quit. They worked hard for it. It wasn't easy and it wasn't a fast payoff. And this develops their character.

TO HEAR MORE, VISIT DEADLYVIPER.ORG

Chapter 4

The Assassin of The Headless Sprinting Chicken

IF YOU TRUST ME COMPLETELY, I CAN HELP YOU.
IF I TELL YOU, YOU ARE NOT WITHIN A PRISON,
THE PRISON IS WITHIN YOU, CAN YOU BELIEVE THAT?
– CAINE, *KUNG FU*

Meet our friend, Matt. Today, he sits in the coffee shop looking like he's slept on the street for a few days. Maybe he has.

No one around us has a clue that six months ago, this guy appeared to be a very with-it CEO. Six months ago, he was a recognized young leader with magazines and cable news interviews under his belt. Matt was the corporate rock star incarnate.

That was then; this is now.

Today, he has bags hung under his brown eyes. His hair is ruffled by more than the wind from a weekend cruise. His clothes look like they're circa 1990 Seattle warehouse grunge. Right now they smell like they haven't been laundered since then, either.

Yeah, this brother has really let himself go. But why? Matt tells us about eighty-hour work weeks. He talks about the constant pressure to perform and the relentless and unbearable schedule he keeps. (He's beginning to make us feel mega-anxious, like a very large shoe is about to drop.) Then, like he's confessing a crime, he shares how he devised his own ruin.

After seven years of pushing hard and leading a large organization, he began to fantasize about getting out. He tried to resign. The organization pressured him to stay. They upped his pay. They did the Godfather bit and "made him an offer he couldn't refuse."

The pay made up for the craziness for a little while, but eventually he decided to execute the "final solution." He'd lie to his organization. He'd have an affair on his wife. No real reason for it either, except to get out. Those two acts would end every relationship that demanded anything from him. The organization would terminate him. No more offers to stay on and, for sure, no more expectations. His wife would despise him – but not just for the affair. That would simply give her the excuse she needed to end the pain she'd been living with because of him.

What a plan! Isn't it amazing how fatigue and exhaustion can cloud a very smart person's judgment? Let's just say he's succeeded on all fronts. Today, he lives with immeasurable regret and heartache. He'd do anything to go back and do things differently, but he feels it's too late. His voice exudes a sense of impending doom. He's too tired for it to sound like anything else.

Matt is fried. Exhausted. Emotionally and physically burnt out, with his spiritual and mental parts soon to follow.

盟 RUN, BABY, RUN

Ever feel like you're sliding into a meltdown? On a bad roller coaster ride headed for the crazy farm? Ever feel like the demands on your life are simply unsustainable? Just to get a break from the madness that is your life, do you find yourself caught up in some destructive patterns of escapism and fantasy?

If so, you just might have booked yourself an appointment with the Assassin of the Headless Sprinting Chicken. He'll beat you to a pulp, lop your head off, and take nunchucks to your loved ones all while you buzz around from one manic appointment to another. You'll be found in a corner curled up in the fetal position, a headless twitch. He won't even break a sweat.

Think Bruce Lee meets Hannibal Lecter. The scary thing about this assassin is if it has his way with you, you may never be the same again. You can run around in the whirl of productivity and busyness and fry yourself to the point of no return, sort of like a bad acid trip that never ends.

Tom is a forty-three-year-old dentist who rocks at what he does. He has a waiting list for future patients, a loving wife, and two adolescent sons who kick butt at Guitar Hero for XBox 360. But eventually, Tom pushed so hard

WATCH YOUR BACK...

HE'LL BEAT YOU TO A PULP, LOP YOUR HEAD OFF,
AND TAKE NUNCHUCKS TO YOUR LOVED ONES, ALL
WHILE YOU BUZZ AROUND FROM ONE MANIC
APPOINTMENT TO THE NEXT.

for so long that he went into a severe depression. The doctor now tells him his serotonin levels are shot, that he's basically baked his brain, and he may never be able to thrive again without medication. He says he now walks with an emotional limp and isn't able to work at the level he could previously. It has affected his whole family.

Jon is a seasoned journalist who pounded the beat for many years for the likes of the *New York Times*. He pushed himself to the max in the madness of Manhattan and amid the most intense of journalistic environments. He didn't pace himself or set any boundaries until a heart attack altered his health so significantly he felt forced to relocate and change career paths. (At least he's still around!)

This Headless Sprinting Chicken Assassin is real. He's dangerous. He's out to inflict hard-core damage.

来 MORE THAN BALANCE

This is probably the point where you'd predict that we'd start talking about finding blissful balance in your life. Just ease up on the accelerator. Find the Zen state waiting to emerge in your schedule. Do yoga twice a week, and cleanse your colon quarterly. Then you'll be swell and destined for greatness.

Think again.

We believe the concept of "balance in life" is the stuff of shrinks and horribly idealistic consultants.

was Van Gogh balanced?

We believe the concept of "balance in life" is the stuff of shrinks and horribly idealistic consultants. Was Van Gogh balanced? The guy cut off his ear, for crying out loud. Or how about our childhood hero, Evel Knievel? Come on, what could be more unbalanced than breaking every bone in your body? It's just a fact that successful and significant people simply aren't the picture of sanitized stability and balance. They are passionate people who have the distinct willingness to do whatever it takes to accomplish a goal. And much good comes from this. Van Gogh's art has inspired millions. His *Café Terrace at Night* hung on Jud's wall for years and brought inspiration and hope. People like Mother Teresa were not balanced, but were passionate about their mission and the world is a much better place because of it.

For years the two of us tried to have lives characterized by what some experts are still calling "balance." We endeavored to achieve all our goals at once: career goals, family goals, fitness goals, spiritual goals. We could keep all the plates spinning for a while, but eventually they'd come crashing down.

It was an incredibly exhausting experience to try to keep every area of our lives firing on all eight cylinders, all the time. We'd have a balanced week, then log two unbalanced weeks gutting it out. Then we'd feel guilty two weeks after that for working so hard and neglecting another area of life. We placed crazy demands on ourselves that nobody else was really asking of us.

Then one day we read an eye-opening and liberating article in *Fast Company* by Keith Hammonds. Read and savor the following:

The truth is, balance is bunk.

The words seemed so prophetic. "For those of us trying desperately to keep up with everything that needs doing, it poses two mythical ideals. If we work hard enough at it, one goes, we can have everything. Or if we cut back, we can have just enough to be truly content. The first obliges us to accomplish too much, often at too high a price; the second doesn't let us accomplish enough."[5]

亲 YOUR PORTFOLIO

Hammonds challenged us to see life as a portfolio of chapters. The goal is not to be balanced perfectly all the time, but to look at one's entire life portfolio. There will be chapters filled with very intense work. Other chapters will be more consumed with family time, and still other chapters with relaxation.

We're all for hard work and hours spent in meaningful tasks that help others. Leaders think about their jobs often. We think that's a good thing. Frankly, we're tired of being beat up by seminars and do-gooders that talk about balance, but in the end imply we should be less passionate about our work. We're idealistic. We're trying to change the world. Of course we're going to be incredibly passionate about what we do! It matters! So catch this thought by Keith Hammonds:

> **Balance is a relic, a fleeting phenomenon of a closed, industrial economy that doesn't apply in a global, knowledge-based world.**

The danger of burnout comes when our priorities are not clear and aligned. Then, we can sacrifice the best, most important things for things that are merely good. We can completely lose ourselves in a task to the point that our emotional and physical gauges hit empty. This is when we make poor leadership decisions and often do things that aren't wise. The question is, "How do we position our life in a way that honors our priorities and is sustainable over the long haul?"

快 LEAD YOURSELF. NO ONE ELSE WILL.

Jud here. Years ago I sat down for lunch with a leader I admired and respected. I felt overwhelmed with my current job responsibilities, yet my responsibilities were nothing compared to his.

I began to whine about all I had to do and all that was going on. I assumed he'd lob me some compassion and friendly counsel. Stupid me. Instead, he put his fork down, swallowed his pasta, and said in a sharp tone, "Grow up! If you are going to be a leader, you have to learn to lead yourself. So, lead yourself." Then he took another bite.

I sat stunned. I felt like I had been slapped in the face. And the worst part about it—he was right on. I needed that. In fact, it changed my life in a positive way. When my reserves are low, I don't blame my circumstances, my job, my employer, or anyone else. I blame myself.

I am responsible to lead myself, to ensure that I'm resting, learning, growing, and bringing my very best self to the job every day. I'm the only one who knows what my emotional, physical, and spiritual gauges are telling me, and I've got to listen to them. I am responsible for my own self-care, growth, and development.

The truth is, I've sucked at this for much of my life. From the time I overheard my wife say to a friend on the phone one night that she felt like a single mom because I was always gone, either physically or emotionally, to the time my six-year-old daughter said, "Dad, I wish you weren't a pastor," as I was heading out the door to help someone else in crisis. My lessons in this area have come through failure and difficulty. I've learned that busy is not bad, but we have to be busy about the best things.

To guard against the Assassin of the Headless Sprinting Chicken, Mike and I are diligent about taking a day off each week to rest. We guarantee you will be more effective with a full day of rest than working seven days straight. Sometimes it takes a heroic effort to pull off a full day away from work, but we do it anyway. We leave projects unfinished. We leave emails unanswered that can wait another day.

We've also made it a priority to identify things that fill us up when we feel emotionally, physically, or spiritually tired. Taking in a baseball game while devouring a Super Slugger nachos does wonders for Mike's soul. So does watering his lawn by hand. Jud finds saddling up in his Man Cave with a book written by some dead philosopher does the trick for him. In fact, he will often put a one-hour appointment on his calendar with some dead guy or gal so that he makes time to read and fill up. He treats it like an immovable appointment, as concrete as those appointments with other "living" people. Maybe you find solace in going to a concert, or on a five-mile run. (One other thing: when engaged in these activities, throw your Crackberry or cell phone in the trunk for good measure.)

Perhaps most important in all of this is that we have become okay with disappointing other people. We can't be all things to all people. But we have prioritized our family and our friendships and have become more concerned about not disappointing them. We often strive to be home by 6:00 or 6:30 p.m. and we make time to play with our kids and talk to them about their lives. We've limited the number of nights we have reoccurring commitments, keeping four or five nights a week free for family time. We've tried to find things our kids love, and meet them in those things. For Jud's daughter, it is games like Clue or Monopoly; for Mike's son, it is taking him to the Star Wars Convention recently.

We try to listen to our bodies, minds, friends, and family. We have to be very in touch with how much we can process or take. We get plenty of sleep.

We aren't opposed to seeing the counselor or some coach. In fact, we think everybody should do some "couch time" at some point on the journey.

Maybe your own health plan—starting today, for the long haul—is a good idea for you. You could start by asking questions about how much you work and who pays the price for your commitment. Do your friends and family ever see you? Is your pace sustainable for the long haul? Make a list of the top five people in your life. Find out how those individuals feel. People are what matter most in our lives, so prioritize time for them. The second wealthiest person in the world, Warren Buffett, once said: "If people get to my age and they have the people love them that they want to have love them, they're successful. It doesn't make any difference if they've got a thousand dollars in the bank or a billion dollars in the bank."[6] Have you built time for those who you want to love you? This will not happen without commitment.

We need to push it to the limit, but not beyond the limit. If we are going to be engaged in furious work, then we also need to be engaged in furious rest (as our friend Louie Giglio calls it).

Effective leaders know leadership is about the long haul. It's not just about a short season of greatness where you burn hot and then burn out. We're tired of seeing too many young leaders being scraped up off the concrete after getting pummeled by the Assassin of the Headless Sprinting Chicken. Don't become another victim.

DILIGENT AND DISCIPLINED

You need to be as diligent and disciplined about ways you recover and rest as you are about how you stress and make a contribution to your work.

- Marcus Buckingham

WISDOM FROM A MASTER

MARCUS BUCKINGHAM

Founder of
The Marcus Buckingham Company.

Bestselling author of
Now, Discover Your Strengths and
The One Thing You Need To Know.
He has sold over three million books.

Expert trainer and speaker
on outstanding leadership
and management practices.

Thought leader
of the "strengths revolution."

WHAT WOULD YOU SAY TO SOMEONE WHO HAS MADE CHARACTER MISTAKES?

The great thing about character is that it's a choice. You can choose whether you are going to be there for somebody else. Everyone's shoulders are broad in different areas and if you've been blowing chunks in one area, maybe, just maybe, it's because you've been in areas where you aren't very broad shouldered at all.

And you've been failing, and your self-esteem has been dropping, and your self-love has been dropping. You've been in situations repeatedly where you have been expected to have broad shoulders and you don't. Perhaps one of the smartest ways for you to be the best with yourself and other people is for you to take responsibility and figure out where you have broad shoulders.

Leadership is about knowing what you can rely on other people for and what people can rely on you for. Leaders are not well rounded, and their greatest achievement is knowing where they are strongest by knowing where they can carry the most people on their back.

ON DEVELOPING CHARACTER...

I think so much of character is making it right. If I'm late for lunch with you I don't say, "I'm sorry, it was the traffic." I say, "I'm sorry, it's the traffic, I'm buying you lunch." It's silly. But that's what restitution is. You make it right!

I think so much of what it takes to gain other people's trust is the realization of when it doesn't go right, you make it right. There is restitution. Confessing you made a mistake is an adolescent level of authenticity. That's nice. We like that. But the adult level of authenticity is you are going to make it right. We don't see that enough.

TO HEAR MORE, VISIT DEADLYVIPER.ORG

Chapter 5

The Assassin of

Boom Chicka Wah Wah

YOU DON'T KNOW WHO IS SWIMMING NAKED
UNTIL THE TIDE GOES OUT.
– WARREN BUFFETT

Honor is a virtue in many martial arts systems. Not just honor in battle, but honor in relationships. The thinking goes, if the student can honor relationships, the student can honor the commitments of training and study to advance through the ranks.

This wisdom not only makes sense in the martial arts. It also makes sense in our lives. When relationships and families fall apart, so does performance at work. So it becomes impossible to talk about character assassins without talking about sexuality and commitments. If you're a human being with blood pumping through your body, you're potentially easy pickings. In fact, how you express your sexual desire affects your significance and your success over the long haul. Tangibly. In fact, some consulting services estimate that a divorce has a monetary cost to the workplace – perhaps the equivalent of one and a half year's worth of salary and benefits. Not to mention the personal pain and heartache.

京 I BE CONCUBINING

Our world has all kinds of views on sex, doesn't it? If you have traveled internationally you've seen this diverse approach. From Islamic countries to the beaches of the French Riviera, we approach sex differently. Comedian

Yakov Smirnoff once said, "I like American women. They do things sexually that Russian girls never dream of doing – like showering."

Yakov might be a little off on that one, but here is what the research shows about our views on sex. Russians never say "nyet," the French don't think affairs are that big of a deal, and the Japanese consider sexing it up to be a form of recreation. Then there is Kazakhstan, with the lowest infidelity rate in the world. And we Americans have twenty-five-year-old Ricky Lackey, a Cincinnati record producer, who a year ago had six babies on the way. While appearing in court, a judge asked him how many children he had.

"None, but I have six on the way," he answered.

"Are you marrying a woman with six children?" asked the confused judge.

"No, I be concubining," Ricky replied.

Yes Ricky, you certainly have been concubining.

Whether you've been sexing it up like our record producer or just walking a little too close to the edge, this assassin is out there ready to trip you up. The hormones get raging. An innocent lunch meeting turns into dessert in the back seat of the Chrysler. A night of celebration with a colleague on a business trip can lead to a night of pleasure. A few drinks, a few thousand miles from home, and Boom Chicka Wah Wah.

The 1000 Mile Rule

Salespeople call it the One Thousand Mile Rule. Within one thousand miles of home, you play by the rules and don't fool around. Beyond one thousand miles, you feel like you can do whatever you want.

—*USA Today* Article on Infidelity

Is this serious stuff? You better believe it. Recently in a span of ten days, Mike knew seven different people lose their leadership positions because of this assassin. Sexuality is powerful and mysterious. It is not quite tame in any of us. We must honestly respect its influence in our lives.

美 XXX

It's Mike. I've been on a fairly unconventional journey when it comes to the issue of sex. I referred earlier to an organization called XXXchurch. That's a venture I founded in 2002. It helps people who are spinning out of control with their sexuality. One of our XXXchurch activities has been to set up booths at sex trade shows and porn conventions and counsel people. The time that I've spent helping people in the sex industry gave me a very clear perspective on the good, the bad, and the very ugly side of sex.

In our booth, I would talk with porn-lovers. I'd hand out helpful information, while my wife would wear the XXXchurch mascot suit, Rex the Rabbit. This wasn't a Playboy bunny outfit! This was a full-blown head to toe rabbit costume that sort of looked like the Easter bunny you would see at your local mall. Having my wife with me made such a huge difference in my personal accountability. Even though she hated wearing the hot and stinky rabbit costume, she was an incredible supporter of the cause.

At some of these porn conventions, over sixty thousand people would show up and buy a fifty dollar ticket to the adult version of Disneyland. Fans would wait in hour-long lines to meet porn stars, get autographs, and take raunchy pictures. And if you were so inclined, you could purchase a ten thousand dollar sex android to take home with you.

When I say I've seen it all, I really mean it.

While at the shows, we encountered some of the most broken and sexually messed-up people I have ever met. Their sexuality was out of control. Instead of them having power over sex, sex was controlling and ultimately breaking them.

After a speaking engagement in Indiana, I met Dan. He was a 6'5" football-type guy in his fifties, who was dressed in a two-thousand-dollar suit. As he came up to me, Dan started to sob uncontrollably and break down. After about five minutes of weeping, Dan was starting to freak me out a little.

When he finally composed himself, he told me his story. He shared how he was a successful president of a major university, married for twenty-four years, and financially well off, but all that had changed six months earlier. Dan explained that he was caught in an FBI sting trying to hook up with a thirteen-year-old online. His idiotic and illegal decision left him facing a seven-year prison term. It all came crashing down in a moment. Score one for the Assassin of Boom Chicka Wah Wah.

乐 NOT ABOUT SEX

One of the things we've discovered as we reflect on conversations with thousands of people about sex is that sexual missteps are rarely about sex. They're really about our desire for a deep, meaningful, and powerful connection with someone.

Our friend Rob says that many times our sexuality is our awareness of how profoundly we're severed, cut off, and disconnected from each other. In those situations, males often feel relationally emasculated. Women feel emotionally barren. He believes our sexuality is an expression of all of the ways we go about trying to reconnect.

A recent survey backed up Rob's observation. It shows that the major factor contributing to extramarital relationships is physical and emotional connection (78%), which far outdistanced marital dissatisfaction (41%). Dodging the Boom Chicka Wah Wah Assassin isn't really about dodging sex, then. It's about nurturing the right relationships.

际 A PORSCHE OR A VOLVO?

And relationships take a lot of work and care, don't they? We have a consultant friend who, along with his wife, has discovered a huge insight about their relationship. "My wife and I have realized our marriage is a Porsche, not a Volvo. It has all the high-end performance you could ever want, but it needs high maintenance, too. It needs to go into the shop for diagnostics' tests and tune-ups. We have to take really good care of it. We can't neglect it. It's not a Ford or a Chevy. We've got to spend time together on a regular, frequent basis. It has to be time with just the two of us and no kids. Otherwise we know this Porsche isn't going to run very well and will eventually break down.

We go for a glass of wine together often. We try to get away together overnight a couple of times a year. We need our date nights."

What about your relationships? Which ones are Fords? Which ones are Porsches? Are you treating them according to their needs?

年 WHAT'S MY SCORE?

Recently we went out on a double date with our wives to Sammy's Woodfired Pizza. We know how to treat our women right. Sammy's is cheap, they give you free bread, and you can watch a ballgame on TV. But the most important thing about this pizza joint is our wives really dig the place and like going there. It was the perfect spot for great conversations and to just hang.

As we sat there chatting about life, kids, and our favorite reality shows, the conversation turned toward marriage. We often talk about our wives and how we want to be better husbands but this conversation was different. This time the marriage conversation had our wives present and, as you might have guessed, that raised the stakes. No fudging, no embellishing, no spinning of the facts. Our wives wouldn't allow it in any shape or form.

If you haven't figured it out by now, you can BS all you want to your colleagues, employees, congregations, friends, and buddies, but there is no BSing your spouse. Spouses are great at keeping us real and keeping it authentic. We can honestly attest to the fact that our lovely ladies are pretty unimpressed with all the things that others seem to fancy about us. And that is a very good thing.

SO IS
YOUR RELATIONSHIP A

OR A

ARE YOU CONSISTENTLY ASKING FOR EVALUATION IN HOW YOU ARE DOING IN YOUR RELATIONSHIP?

WHAT DO YOU THINK YOUR SCORE WOULD BE?

{ WHAT'S YOUR SCORE? }

So here we were in a little pizza joint waiting for our five-cheese pizza and our Caesar salad, chatting about life. Nice conversations. Nice free bread. Just a "nice" little dialogue. But then the "nice" conversation turned into a real conversation when Jud threw down the gauntlet. He asked Lori to honestly and truthfully rate their marriage on a scale of one to ten. He wanted to know how he was doing. Good or bad, he wanted to know. As the saying goes, "cruelties should be committed all at once," and he wanted to get it all out there. So the results came in and Lori gave Jud an eight and a half. We were all pretty impressed with Jud's husband score and then we talked about why Lori gave him that grade. Getting home on time, listening better, and really pitching in around the house had garnered some big points for the Judster.

Then out of sheer enthusiasm or sheer stupidity, Mike decided to ask his wife to rate their marriage. If Jud is man enough to ask this bold question then Mike should be brave enough too. So Mike looked at his wife and asked, "What's my score? How do you rate our marriage? What grade do I get as a husband? Be very honest." Jennifer paused, then gave me a solid eight. Which we must point out is something akin to a B minus and less than Jud's score, but still an overall good grade and Mike felt relieved and gratified.

So, set aside the issue of the scores for a moment – and our collective relief that they didn't give us fives, which we've certainly deserved at various moments in our marriages. What score we got isn't really the point of recounting this story. What is important is that in this tiny pizza place in downtown San Diego a very important character thing happened. Four people got honest about dealing with the true status of their relationships. We asked a hard question. And to be quite frank, when we ask for these honest revelations it can easily go two ways, can't it?

On this particular evening we came out winners. But we know firsthand that isn't always how it unfolds. Either way, though, these moments lend us a clear snapshot of how we're doing in one of the most important areas of our lives. Asking for this analysis shows strength and depth of character. It's the warrior's way. Avoiding these conversations shows weakness and will eventually lead to the truth being revealed in more unfortunate ways.

We need to be purposeful with our relationships. Don't simply wish that your key relationships will be okay. They take effort, sacrifice, passion, and focus just like our work does. And make no mistake, there will be a direct correlation between how high you fly in leadership and how strong and deep your relationships are.

明 THE BIG GNARLY CHOICE

The fact is, we're always looking for shortcuts. So hear this: In the case of countering the measures employed by the Assassin of Boom Chicka Wah Wah, there are no shortcuts or Cliff's Notes versions. You need to draw thick, thoughtful boundaries to protect your relationships and your reputations. Sometimes, even the smallest flub-up or oversight in this area can take us down:

- A sexual harassment accusation, true or false, could change everything.
- Being caught downloading inappropriate material online can really damage you.
- Visiting the local strip joint, even for a friend's bachelor or bachelorette party, could have some damaging leadership consequences.

So let's get mondo practical here.

You see, many people will have the opportunity to hop into the sack with someone inappropriately. You will have the opportunity to cross a line sexually. You will be faced with a situation that looks like you just can't pass up. It's not if, it's when. So unless you want to be plundered by the Boom Chicka Wah Wah Assassin, you'd better be prepared to make a good decision.

As two guys who are just like you, we know we must be prepared ourselves. We're not idiots. We know we'll be tempted. Everyone will be faced with difficult choices in this area. We are committed to making sure that we make great choices in regards to our sexuality.

for

a

good

time

call

deadlyviper.org

忍者武士暗殺者

家 BE PREPARED BEFOREHAND

Kata is a Japanese word meaning "pattern" or "form." In karate terms, a kata is a prescribed sequence of techniques against an imagined opponent. You develop techniques and predefined moves before you ever face a real, in-the-flesh enemy. In other words, you prepare beforehand. We brainstorm the ways this assassin may ambush us. And we steel ourselves in advance. We mentioned our traveling with a friend, but here is another: When we are on a business trip, we leave our homes on the latest flight possible and come back home on the earliest flight possible. We don't hang out. We get in and we get out. We minimize the time away from home. It's a good plan. Again, the important thing is not that your plan looks like ours, but that you have a plan to begin with.

民 STARTING OVER

So maybe you've been reading this chapter and think, "I wish I could start all over again in this area." Perhaps you have made some poor choices and no matter how hard you work, you feel like the scarlet letter is plastered permanently on your chest. Don't worry; you're not alone in that feeling. Seasons of regret are part of every life journey, but it certainly doesn't have to be that way forever.

There is no question in our minds that you can beat this assassin in the future. You can grow into a rhythm of healthy choices. You can saddle up with your guilt, beat yourself up over your shortcomings, or you can be a true samurai and begin anew. Grasshopper, we all need to cut ourselves some slack when it comes to our past performance in this area. Alice Abrams said that, "In life as in dance: Grace glides on blistered feet." It's time to glide, young warrior.

SEXUALITY

is powerful and mysterious.
It is not quite tame in any of us.
We must honestly respect its
influence in our lives.

CRAIG GROESCHEL

Senior Pastor of LifeChurch.tv which has over twenty thousand people in attendance at their weekend services.

Bestselling author of Chazown and Confessions of a Pastor.

Married for seventeen years with six kids.

HOW DO YOU CULTIVATE CHARACTER IN YOUR STAFF?

Character is worked into everything we do at LifeChurch. We work very strategically at integrating integrity and transparency into the culture of our staff. If you don't intentionally do it, it doesn't happen. So from day one both with our staff and with the church those are topics we talk about over and over again.

So how this works practically with our staff is that we start with the whole staff. I talk about this almost on a monthly basis. We also address it in smaller groups and in their teams. Also, everyone on our staff has a partner that they are accountable to.

WHAT SHOULD LEADERS DO IF THEY HAVE FAILED IN THE ISSUE OF CHARACTER?

First, for leaders who make mistakes, there must be a full confession—that's necessary. Sometimes in trying to save the person who has fallen the church tries to bury the truth. Then what happens is the rumors become worse than the truth. I'm passionate about this because one of my mentors had a moral failure and the church didn't say what he did. He had an affair. Though the rumors were he had an affair, he stole from the church, and that he was gay. Things that were just not true. He never got counseling and he never fully confessed. So what happened? He killed himself.

I'm almost reluctant to talk about it because I don't want to curse it but in eleven years we have had only one moral failure. And it was a guy who came from another church and six weeks into his time with us he confessed because the culture was so transparent and the accountability was so high. He was personally convicted and so he came and confessed to the affairs. He resigned with integrity and three years later was restored to ministry. Now he serves as a regional campus pastor and has a great marriage. It became a tremendous success story. But we went public and stopped the rumors with the truth. It is out and he will tell you it helped him. It's the hard and fast rule—some would debate me. I think a partial confession is dangerous. A full confession is what is appropriate. A truthful confession helps you live a more authentic life.

TO HEAR MORE, VISIT DEADLYVIPER.ORG

Chapter 6

the bling bling
assassin

RE-EXAMINE ALL YOU HAVE BEEN TOLD.
DISMISS WHATEVER INSULTS YOUR OWN SOUL.
– WALT WHITMAN

The overwhelming majority of martial arts weaponry finds its genesis in ancient oriental farm tools. Today's nunchucks, for example, have barely changed from the farm tools used to thresh grain in the Orient. Bos (long staffs) can be traced to the rods once used to carry buckets of water and herd cattle. Kamas still look much like the short sickles used for harvesting generations ago.

These farm implements, in an instant, would be used by simple farmers to protect their villages and families from raiders. Although it was to your advantage to know how to use a variety of such weaponry, there is a simple principle of the universe that is as applicable today as it was centuries ago: A person has but two hands.

In ancient times, farmers under attack had no time (and usually no resources) to load their arms with weapons. They had to be ready with what they had, not what they wished they had.

The need to optimize their existing resources kept the farmer-warriors focused. It resulted in exceptional expertise in the use of the tools that became weapons when necessary. Because the farmer had but two hands, he felt no need to burden himself with extra things that would limit his mobility.

Our material-obsessed culture could learn a lot from those simple farmers, couldn't we? These farmers were resourceful and courageous. They weren't sitting around on eBay looking for better, newer, or fancier weapons.

来 MOVING TOWARD ENOUGH

When is enough really enough? How much do you need to be happy? It's a pretty good question, and one that we rarely pause to consider.

We recently read a fact that Americans spend more annually on trash bags than nearly half the world's population spends on all goods.

There's no doubt our society is subjected to non-stop product marketing and advertising. We're obsessed with the newest, the shiniest, and the most conspicuous. We're inundated with opportunities to buy, upgrade, and accumulate.

Case in point: just between these two authors, we personally own a total of six iPods. And no, we are not making this up. (Like we said, we're on the same journey you're on.)

But, a true person of character must manage this tension between money and worth. Grasshopper, we must hold things loosely and learn to be more generous with our possessions.

亲 YOUR POSSESSIONS DO NOT SHOW WORTH

Unfortunately, a lot of us have come to believe that our possessions, bank accounts, and salaries determine our worth. We're all caught up in this really brutal game of "keeping up with the Joneses." Is it new? Then great! Is it big and expensive? Even better! If it makes me look like the winner in life's pursuit of the most toys, then I. Must. Possess. It.

If this wasn't the case, why would we buy bigger houses, faster cars, or receive the endless supply of credit card offers in the mail? Why would we need Skymall, either? You all know Skymall, right? It's that incredible "retailer in the sky." It gives airline travelers – the consumer at forty thousand feet – the opportunity to purchase some garden tools, or a Lord of the Rings sword, or a nose hair trimmer. Admit it. Like the rest of us, you've been tempted at some time in a flight to place an order for that doggie ladder or remote control blimp. Skymall realizes that we like to buy stuff, especially when we're bored stiff on a five-hour flight to New York.

临 PHILOSOPHY OF ACCUMULATION

This philosophy of accumulation has slowly and subversively crept into our souls. Quite frankly, it is taking us to a scary place – the very place where the Bling Bling Assassin can do his best work on us. Consider these few startling findings:

- Last year more people filed for bankruptcy than graduated from college.
- Finances are a key factor in 90% of divorces.

- In Los Angeles, pet owners can spend two thousand dollars on their pooch for a doggie rhinoplasty. Friends, that's two grand for a nose job for Sparky.
- And by the way, since we're on conspicuous canine consumption (say that fast five times without stopping), for fifty bucks you can pick up an oatmeal body wrap at LA Dogworks, an exclusive spa for canines.

Are we insane? Yes. Are we being influenced to make stupid choices when it comes to our money and priorities? Absolutely!

家 BRING SOME DEFINITION TO THE DEBT PROBLEM

How do we fund our philosophy of accumulation. Well, through debt of course. Debt is a key strategy of the Bling Bling Assassin. But here's what our friendly neighborhood thesaurus says when she talks about the word "debt":

- obligation
- encumbrance
- in the red
- pound of flesh
- beaten down
- unable to keep the wolf from the door

- hard up
- bound
- strapped
- fleeced
- busted

Get the picture?
Nothing pretty about it, is there?

Real Success in life means the individual's conquest of himself; it means how he has bettered himself, not how he has bettered his fortune. The great question in life is not "What have I?" but "What am I?"

– William George Jordan

举 JUNKY CAR CLUB

Last year, Mike came to realize he was slowly becoming a prize candidate for the Bling Bling Assassin's mantelpiece. He was driving around in an amazingly sweet $50,000 sports car. He loved it. It had the premium Bose sound system, navigation, leather interior, and high-end rims and tires. It was a status symbol of his success in his career. He felt a lot of attachment to the car. He loved the way he felt taking potential clients to lunch in it. He loved the personalized license plate that read IDEABOY.

The vehicle was an advertisement for a guy who's totally on top of his game. But one day Mike began to catch on that his attachment to this car and his weird ideas about it were just plain stupid. Walt Whitman said it with these sage words: "Re-examine all you have been told; dismiss whatever insults your own soul."

That's exactly what Mike did. He dismissed what was insulting his soul and ditched the sports car. He now happily drives a 1993 Camry with 130,000 miles and a radio that buzzes as you accelerate. As an added bonus, the car even has a funky smell on hot days.

About a year later Mike started an organization called the Junky Car Club. The club encourages others to live with less so they can give more to those who are in need. He recruits his friends and anyone else

join the revolution

living with less so we can give more.

wanting to rebel against out of control consumerism. (Interested? Visit www.JunkyCarClub.com to join.) Sure, Mike's kids always request to ride in Mommy's car (a GMC Denali). They're painfully embarrassed by Daddy's car. But Mike gave the Bling Bling Assassin a good boot in the behind when he unloaded his sports car.

际 ARE NICE THINGS NOT NICE?

Now let's be clear here: There's nothing wrong with having nice things. However, there *is* something wrong with drawing personal value or self worth from your stuff. If you think for one split millisecond that your possessions will define you as a significant person, think again.

There is no question that if you want to be someone who discovers meaning in life, you must tame this beast. As healthy people we must strategically think about how we can be more generous and sacrificial. We can use our financial assets for positive things.

We can attain a healthy perspective. Too often we ignore wisdom for our own materialistic drives. We do some really boneheaded things. We use credit like there's no tomorrow. We eat up expense accounts and screw the rank and file out of Christmas bonuses. We buy for the sake of looking good, rather than for the sake of real enjoyment.

And in so doing, we leave ourselves wide open for this assassin to fillet our fiscal fish.

So ask yourself:

- How satisfied are you with your income, house size, or possessions?
- How many times during the day do you think about what you want versus what you could give?
- How much personal value or self worth do you find in what you own?
- What percentage of your income are you giving away to help others?

These questions lead us to the big money question (yep, literally) for each one of us: How much is enough?

明 THE ENOUGH FACTOR

In their book, *Your Money or Your Life*, Joe Dominguez and Vicki Robin refer to a research project involving one thousand people. The participants were asked to rate their happiness on a scale of one (miserable) to five (joyous), with three being "can't complain."

Dominguez and Robin then correlated the participants' answers to their incomes. Their research shows that a certain amount of possessions can make us happy and satisfied. However, our tendency is to think that the more we have the more satisfaction we will experience. (You know the line: "If I had more than I have now, then I would be happy.") But the reality is the opposite. The research suggests that the more we have beyond a certain amount, the more our satisfaction actually decreases.

This is groundbreaking stuff. This is the stuff of revolution.

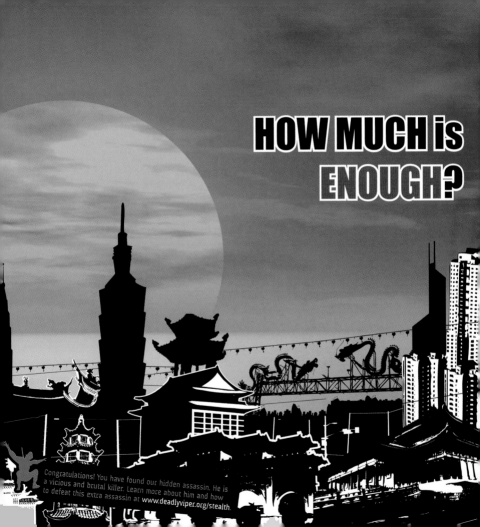

HOW MUCH is ENOUGH?

Congratulations! You have found our hidden assassin. He is a vicious and brutal killer. Learn more about him and how to defeat this extra assassin at www.deadlyviper.org/stealth.

Dominguez and Robin call the place where our satisfaction and our stuff come together "enough."[7] It is simply enough.

We all need to define what "enough" is for us.

And consider this: Americans' personal income has increased more than two and a half times over the last fifty years, but their happiness level has remained the same. And you thought the rich were a lot happier. Not exactly. Americans earning more than ten million annually are only slightly happier than average Americans.[8] We don't know about you, but we feel better knowing we are as happy as millionaires. As Warren Buffett often reminds us: the average college student lives more comfortably today than millionaire John Rockefeller ever did. The college student has all the modern comforts of heating, air conditioning, entertainment, etc. Not to mention Top Ramen.

快 LOTTERY AND THE LOSERS

We are all familiar with the tragic stories of the lottery winners who win millions only to have their lives impacted in a negative way. Jack Whittaker woke up on Christmas morning in 2002 and learned he had won the Powerball Lottery Jackpot of $315 million. So why would Jack now say that he wishes he'd never won the lottery? Well, first came the requests for money and help from friends and strangers. He gave away fifty million dollars worth of cars, cash, and houses. Then the lawsuits started piling on where Whittaker had over four hundred legal claims against him and his company. The lawyer bills reached three million just to defend himself.

Jack became depressed and started drinking heavily and withdrew from life. He also made the mistake of giving enormous amounts of money to his seventeen-year-old granddaughter, Brandi. Cars and cash would bring the same set of problems to this seventeen-year-old. Brandi would eventually start using drugs and two years after winning the Powerball Lottery, Jack lost his granddaughter to a drug overdose. He calls the $315 million win a curse.

明 THE TRIPLE BOTTOM LINE (TBL)

We love Mark Zuckerberg, the twenty-two-year-old founder of Facebook. (Of course, we're a bit envious too.) It is reported that he turned down one billion dollars for the purchase of his social networking company because he loves what he is doing. He realized if he took the billion dollars then he would no longer be in charge and the vision he had for his venture would likely be totally corrupted and dishonored in the buyer's appetite for profits.

Zuckerberg recently said that we all should "focus on something we think is important rather than trying to start a company just to make money. We need to come up with things that would make an impact and be valuable to the world."

none of us is as
smart as all of us.

– japanese proverb

That's some great wisdom coming from a twenty-two-year-old. Mark is a dangerous warrior and we feel sorry for this assassin if he ever goes after him.

We need to focus on the Triple Bottom Line (TBL). This idea can be succinctly described as "People, Planet, and Profit." People come before the bottom line. People, and their gifts, are what we are entrusted with in life. They are what make life rich, textured, and wonderful. Next is the planet. We must be mindful of how our decisions affect the environment both for our age and for future generations. We only have one earth to manage. Then comes profit. If we put profit before people and the planet, we may rake in a lot of money, but we can't enjoy it without healthy relationships (people) and a sustainable environment (planet). It all works together to form the TBL where the ultimate goal is sustainability.

The TBL taps into an expanded spectrum of values and criteria for measuring organizational and social success. This can play out in your life in a variety of ways. But the main point here is that people who think more holistically about financial success are more effective. If you're laser focused on just the bottom line on your Excel spreadsheet in your work and your personal life, you open yourself up to being worked over by the Bling Bling Assassin. And you're going to lose your effectiveness. Maybe your soul.

年 WHAT MATTERS MOST

An edition of *Ode* magazine related some intriguing, instructive results from a ten-year study on near-death experiences directed by Dutch cardiologist Pim Van Lommel.

Van Lommel is regarded as an international expert on near-death experiences, which is to say he has a unique view of what matters most in life.

He says, "Nearly every near-death experience goes hand in hand with a life review during which people gain insight into the consequences of their actions."[9] And what are the results of those life reviews from those fortunate enough to make it back from the edge of the other side? "The life review people experience changes their values," Van Lommel says. "They've seen that it's not about power, appearance, nice cars, clothes, a young body. It's about entirely different things: love for yourself, nature, your fellow human beings."[10]

津 HELPING THOSE IN NEED

So what are some practical things we can do to make sure we are training properly and having correct attitudes about our money, our stuff, and what matters most? We can start by giving to those in need. The average American gives 2% to organizations helping those living in poverty. That's

Every leader has burdens and difficulties and complaints, but nobody forces you into leadership. It is your choice and if you are given it, it is a privilege and a gift. And if you don't feel that way, you should step down. **—Rabbi David Wolpe**

pathetic. As men and women who are striving toward character, this statistic exposes a lack of it.

Jud and Mike are both advocates for Compassion International and, through them, sponsor multiple children who are living in extreme poverty. It's one of the best and most rewarding checks we write every month. You can visit www.DeadlyViper.org or go to www.Compassion.com to join us in sponsoring these kids. You can roll out of your chair, walk over to your computer, do it right now, and land a very satisfying thwack to the Bling Bling Assassin's cranium.

Or how about throwing some of your dough to help the Rwanda Clean Water project? This initiative is helping the people of Rwanda dig wells that spew clean water, which the people there really need. This helps prevent illness, death, and disease that comes from unclean water. One clean well will help approximately seven hundred people have a sustainable clean water solution in their local community. Interested? Go to www.FermiProject.com to learn more.

Each and every one of us has a million options staring us in the face on how we can be more generous and less materialistic. As warriors in training we must pause and sense the next steps. Open your hands and your hearts and you will find what it is to be fully alive, Grasshopper.

Re-examine all
you have been told;
dismiss whatever
insults your soul.

JOE RITCHIE

- One of the most successful option traders in American history.

- Founder of Fox River Financial Resources.

- He has captured four world records in aviation.

JOE, SHARE WITH US YOUR THOUGHTS ON INTEGRITY AND CHARACTER.

I think having great character and integrity is a lot like golf. If you're having a problem with your golf swing, you must first identify the bad swing and then what is causing it. But the cure is not to say don't sway your hips, but to think of a positive. Typically you think about what you WANT to do. When you think about the right things to do with your swing, you automatically stop swinging your hips. Having strong character and making right choices is a very similar scenario.

I also believe that at the end of the day it's about love. If you get love right, then you don't have a taste for those other "bad" things. Character has three different levels in my mind. There are the assassins that get you—that's a negative level. You have to work on those for sure. Then you have the second level of character—having good character. That's good. But then there is the level of love. And when you get it right, all the others fall in place. There's a place for focusing at each of these points but the one you want to arrive at is the one operating from love. Think about the other levels, but you don't want to stay there.

When you see someone living with character, he doesn't look like he's thinking about integrity. He just couldn't do it any other way. When he's on his game, he is just doing it and everything falls in place.

WHAT WOULD YOU SAY TO SOMEONE WHO HAS MADE SOME BAD DECISIONS WHEN IT COMES TO CHARACTER?

That theme is so real. In the trading world, they say all the great traders can go back and tell you exactly where they screwed up and had their back to the wall. They had the wet mustache. And they will tell you that what happened to them was good. That they needed it to happen to them.

I laugh when people talk about the problem of pain and the problem of evil. If there's a God, why is there so much evil? I've got a problem with that. I think if God is good, why should he not allow a lot more of it. It's the only way we seem to learn. I look at myself. I look at the three most painful things that have happened to me in my life and those are the three I wouldn't undo. I believe in hell because I have been there. And that's where you learn everything.

TO HEAR MORE, VISIT DEADLYVIPER.ORG

Chapter 7

the HIGH & MIGHTY ASSASSIN

> THE IMPORTANT THING IS THIS: TO BE ABLE
> AT ANY MOMENT TO SACRIFICE WHAT WE ARE
> FOR WHAT WE WOULD BECOME.
> – CHARLES DU BOIS

Some people are jerks. They are snooty, proud, arrogant, self-absorbed, and high and mighty. They think their job title gives them license to run over other people. They can't see past themselves and blow off the needs of others. They tick me (Jud) off. So it rocked my world to realize other people thought this of me. What were they smoking? Humble little ol' me?

When I was accused of being high and mighty by a coworker, I responded with maturity, "WHO DO YOU THINK YOU ARE TO WALK INTO MY OFFICE AND ACCUSE ME OF BEING ARROGANT? DO YOU KNOW WHO I AM!!??" It really sucked to realize this person was right. I'd enjoyed a little success, picked up a promotion, and I'd allowed it to go to my head. The odd thing about the High and Mighty Assassin is that everyone else knows you've been clobbered by it but you.

Later, I thanked my coworker for having the guts to call me out. His willingness to confront me prompted me to wonder, "Who do I think I am?" That question helped me figure out where I went wrong so I could strive again to treat others with greater respect. Success can ruin your life.

Success can take us to some wonderful places, but it can also take us to some places we don't want to go.

临 PRIDE AND THE PRIMA DONNA IN THE MIRROR

The world is full of enough prima donnas and divas. Sometimes they do what they do in an unhealthy pursuit of proving their worth. They may devalue others to inflate themselves. They may buy into their press reports. But watch out, little diva or divo: the long-term effect of this behavior is not success or health.

Take Nevada District Judge Elizabeth Halverson as an example. Challenged by a variety of weight-related physical issues, Halverson spent nine years as a lowly law clerk for the court. She was eventually fired. Then in 2006, she ran for a judgeship and surprisingly won.

This had all the markings of a success story that could make the daytime talk show circuit. But wait. Apparently, there were even more personality issues than physical issues plaguing the good judge.

Shortly after Halverson took office, reports started coming out of the Regional Justice Center about her shocking egomaniacal behavior toward her staff. According to an article in the *Las Vegas Review-Journal*, Halverson ordered her bailiff to rub her feet and give her back massages. She took delight in throwing her pencil on the floor so she could order the bailiff to pick it up. She called her court clerk "the evil one" and "the

忍者武士暗殺者

Antichrist" and made the staff make her lunch.[11] And you think your boss is a jerk?

It's no wonder that Halverson became the subject of a series of reviews and investigations just a few months into her term as district judge. And when challenged in those processes regarding her behavior, Halverson seemed so full of pride and ego that she couldn't seem to understand why people were so upset.[12] The High and Mighty Assassin had done his work well.

Success never happens in a vacuum. We still have to deal with the people around us—family, friends, coworkers, employees. We'd best remember that in many, many ways, they helped us get where we are. And if we're going to continue successfully, we'll need their help just as much—maybe more.

津 HIGH, MIGHTY, AND MISMATCHED

Now don't get us wrong in all this. A leader can be self-assured and confident. That's way different than being an egotistical jerk that treats people with contempt. In a real way we show people how to treat us by how we treat them. This assassin bases his attack on a false estimation of ourselves.

When we are struck by the High and Mighty Assassin, we can overestimate our giftedness and our chops and our all-that, and find ourselves in real trouble. Many people win promotions due to their past successes and abilities, but

often the new role takes them out of their areas of strength that enabled their success in the first place.

We can't forget our buddy Al who worked for years in a creative agency. Al dazzled others with his phenomenal ideas. He genuinely excelled at being a team player. But when he was promoted to Vice President of Retail Advertising, Al suddenly became the local Creative Nazi. Faster than you can say invasion of the body snatchers, Al's former peers suddenly wondered what happened to the old Al. They paid for disagreeing with Al on projects. Al dished out lousy performance reviews to them. Al started treating assistant staff like they were peasants.

It took the resignation of one of Al's best protégés to wake him up. He handed Al his thirty-day notice with the words, "Al, I don't need your abuse anymore."

Al was too stunned to respond. To his credit, Al took the initiative to remove himself from people management and return to the creative team. It took a few months before he regained the respect he'd lost during his misadventure in management, however.

Appropriate humility is knowing who we are and where we fit and striving to make a difference there.

京 INVERTED PERSPECTIVES

Jud here. I am privileged to lead an organization with more than one hundred and fifty employees. Recently, I tried to create a visual of what was happening in our organization by inverting our organizational chart. I grew weary of seeing myself at the top of the chart with everybody under me, so we inverted every role from the bottom up. I am now lowest on the organization chart. My role is not about entitlement and position. My role is lead servant. I'm here to empower my core leadership team to use their gifts and empower those above them. The most important people in our organization are actually the thousands of volunteers who serve and help the people in our community and those who attend our church. Our success or failure will hinge on those relationships. My questions are not: What can it do for me? But what can I do to serve so that we can all win?

In reality, the chart means nothing if it isn't lived out in the trenches. We are working to make this framework a reality and as we do, I find that our team is accomplishing more than ever before. Pride is being set aside for accomplishing the mission. Honesty about our individual strengths and weaknesses is emerging. We are collaborating and accomplishing dreams. We are working as a team for the greater good.

You may have no say over the organizational chart in the business you work for, but you do have the ability to serve others each day. Every

DO YOU KNOW THE
DREAMS
OF YOUR COWORKERS
AND FRIENDS?

DO YOU KNOW THEIR
FRUSTRATIONS?

DO YOU KNOW THEIR
STRENGTHS?

忍者武士暗殺者

person wants to be known and loved. What would happen if you stopped to talk to three people each day and asked them about their lives? Do you know the dreams of your coworkers and friends? Do you know their frustrations? Do you know their strengths? Have you thought about how you could help them win?

These kinds of questions cripple the High and Mighty Assassin. They lead to the release and sharing of power and influence instead of the hoarding of it. They move people from following us positionally to following us relationally. This is servant leadership at its best.

亲 YO ADRIAN

Awhile back we had the opportunity to meet Sylvester Stallone. Sly was promoting his final Rocky film, *Rocky Balboa*. He talked about his past quite candidly.

Stallone said he got lost in the success of the first four Rocky films. He became arrogant and full of himself. He didn't treat people around him well. He didn't respect others. All of this led to the fifth Rocky film, whimsically entitled *Rocky V*. This movie was ... what's the word? Awful. Stallone admitted it. He said it was the result of his ego. He'd bought into his own PR.

Success ruined the movie, and threatened to ruin his life—but it didn't. Sly went on to share honestly about the positive changes he's made since that movie. He's tried to be more about serving others than being served. He took a hard look in the mirror at who he had become and decided he didn't like what he was seeing. Instead, he basically tried to be more like Rocky – a tough, lovable warrior with a tender heart of gold. Stallone rebounded somewhat with the final movie. He talked of how humbling the process was for him, but how transforming also.

東 DEFENSIVE POSTURES

So how do we parry the tactics of the High and Mighty Assassin? We've found that asking some important questions can help:

- How do others really perceive me?
- Do I listen to others?
- Am I open to learn something from everyone?
- Am I thankful as a person for those who contribute to my success?
- Can I acknowledge my weaknesses as well as my strengths?
- What are my weaknesses?
- When was the last time I admitted I made a bad decision?
- When's the last time I said, "I'm sorry"?
- How often am I the first one to say, "I'm sorry"?

Ask someone you trust how people view you. Dig around until you really find out. The tricky thing about this assassin is that you may be the last to know when he's struck you, and you'll find that everyone else already saw it.

The worst thing is to get that shot and not know what to do with it because you really don't have anything but a desire to be famous.

THAT AIN'T GONNA GET YOU THERE.

And if it does, that's worse. Because if that's all you have...we've seen those meteoric rises, and then you're down the other side.

DON CHEADLE

Actor in *Oceans 11*, *Hotel Rwanda* and author of *Not On Our Watch*.

Empathy and concern for others is one of the most powerful traits of an effective leader.

One way to cultivate a respect for others is to make a list of all the people who helped you get where you are. It could be someone who hired you and gave you a shot. It could include your teachers, your friends, or the client who bought your product or believed in your ability. Write these names down and keep them close by so that you can look at them and remember the importance of other people. Then look around you for someone else to believe in. Make an effort to land on someone else's list of important life influencers. Give someone a shot. Drop someone a note of encouragement. Take someone under your wing and help share what you know.

Don't let the High and Mighty Assassin sneak up on you and destroy your life.

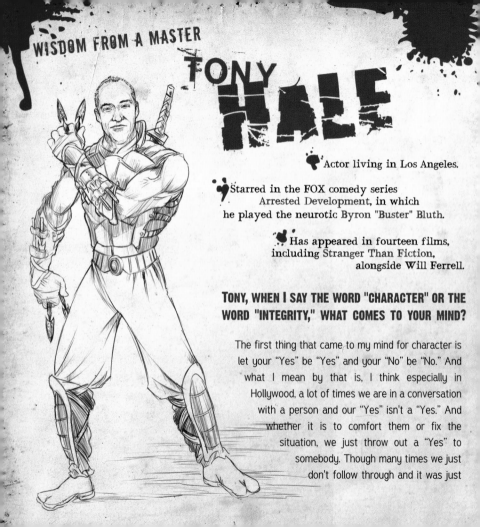

TONY HALE

- Actor living in Los Angeles.

- Starred in the FOX comedy series
  Arrested Development, in which
  he played the neurotic Byron "Buster" Bluth.

- Has appeared in fourteen films,
  including Stranger Than Fiction,
  alongside Will Ferrell.

TONY, WHEN I SAY THE WORD "CHARACTER" OR THE WORD "INTEGRITY," WHAT COMES TO YOUR MIND?

The first thing that came to my mind for character is let your "Yes" be "Yes" and your "No" be "No." And what I mean by that is, I think especially in Hollywood, a lot of times we are in a conversation with a person and our "Yes" isn't a "Yes." And whether it is to comfort them or fix the situation, we just throw out a "Yes" to somebody. Though many times we just don't follow through and it was just to pacify the person. And I think that's the biggest fault in someone's character. If someone follows through with their word, that's huge with me. Many times we don't say "No" to someone for fear that we are going to hurt their feelings or fear that we don't want to seem like a jerk. When in actuality saying "No" is the best thing for them. Mainly, we negate the power of our words. But a person of character realizes how powerful words are.

And let me preface it by saying I've learned this lesson because I've made a lot of mistakes by not letting my "Yes" be "Yes" and my "No" be "No" and I've hurt a lot of people's feelings. "Yes, I'll call you back. Yes, I'll read that script for you. Yes, I'll be there." And then not follow through with any of that. It's sad because our society hasn't valued people's words. And I'd like to be a person who if I say to a person I'll call you later I'll follow through on that.

How would you define what it means to be successful in life?

It's a good practice for everyone to define their definition of success. Your success should be attributed to your significance. They should be together—I don't know if they should be separate. In our society we detach these and they are not together.

I think it is a daily battle because Hollywood is a town where success is determined by what's the latest project. We have to have a certain amount of trophies and a certain amount of climbing the ladder. But if we are being honest, that is going to pass. It's so temporary.

The daily battle for me is that my success is found in my friendships and in my family. It sounds cheesy but it's true. Cause if I based my success on this town, it could change in a week. And if I base my success on that then I might just as well get on medication.

TO HEAR MORE, VISIT DEADLYVIPER.ORG

PEOPLE OF THE
SECOND CHANCE

Chapter 8

THERE IS SO MUCH YOU DON'T KNOW.
AND SO MUCH YOU DO.

– CAINE, *KUNG FU*

So you've gotten through this kung fu crash course on living with integrity. You made it. And we congratulate you. Master Po is pleased.

As we sat in the Man Cave, we thought of closing this book with a clever story, some interesting kung fu tidbits, and some sweet next steps. We decided, however, to bail on that idea.

You see, all of it fell short on what we really wanted to say, the one thing we needed to sear into your brain: Grace. Radical, unrelenting, devastating grace. We want to slug you over the head with grace and have our closing moments together focused on second chances.

We invite you to join us in being People of the Second Chance. It is a radical call to a revolution that occurs in the deepest parts of our souls and in how we treat each other.

Without question, we have sought to inspire you to live a life of radical integrity. But now we want to give you the courage to accept your failures and marinate your mind, heart, soul, emotions, thoughts, and future in grace.

And please, don't fight us on this one. You will be tempted to resist and dismiss us, but don't. You're probably getting ready to rattle off compelling reasons on why you believe you're finished and why your fate is sealed. Put the long list of excuses away. We're not listening.

What if right now, everything we knew and believe about second chances was suddenly turned upside down. Challenged. Tested. No limits. What if we came to realize that everything we thought and believed about love, grace, and forgiveness was wrong?

You see People of the Second Chance is for the

- fired
- incarcerated
- cheats
- philanderers
- crackheads
- losers
- cons

- demoted
- found out
- hypocrites
- marginalized
- crooks
- fakers
- and _____

And yes, that means you because it involves all of us – each and every one of us. Write that vicious thing that still haunts you in the space above. There's grace for that too. No exceptions.

EVERY SAINT HAS A PAST

AND EVERY SINNER HAS A FUTURE.

—Warren Buffett

快 LIMPS AND CRACKS

A couple months ago, I (Mike) was having lunch with my new friend Paul at an Irish pub. Paul is killing it in every way. He lives with integrity and simplicity and is leading a dynamic and successful organization.

I love our emerging friendship and our monthly lunches are always the highlight of my week. So as I devoured my greasy fish and chips, Paul dropped on me this nugget to chew on:

"Mike, I don't trust anyone until I can see their limp."

And I knew exactly what he meant. Our relationship is rich because we've seen each other's limp.

So much of our daily routine is spent putting our best foot forward. We reveal the parts and pieces of our world that have the happy ending, the good stuff. The chapter of our story where we made the right decision, closed the deal, and are the hero.

The reason Paul and I are friends is because we stopped doing that and have connected on the theme of brokenness.

You see, People of the Second Chance embrace the other half of the story, that nagging part of our reality that we work very hard to forget about. The sloppy, uncomfortable, and shameful piece. The story that is hard to

when the rest of the world is walking out the door, your best friends are the ones WALKING IN.

YOU KNOW YOURSELF
BETTER THAN ANYBODY. BUT YOU ARE ALSO
BLIND TO YOURSELF
MORE THAN ANYBODY.

– JOHN ORTBERG

tell. Without question, each one of us has a crack in our integrity that we keep trying, unsuccessfully, to patch.

Consider the words of Leonard Cohen in his song "Anthem":

> **There is a crack, a crack in everything**
> **That's how the light gets in.**

How incredible it would be to sit with you, have a cup of coffee, and reveal to each other the cracks in our lives. Without fear of retribution or condemnation, to pull back the layer of successful wins and show each other our failures. To be safe to share all of it. The mountaintop experiences and the darkest valleys. The home runs and the strikeouts. You want that, don't you? We want that too.

Recently, while speaking to CEOs, we met a man who was highly conflicted as we shared this idea of grace. You see, his story was filled with drug and alcohol addiction that bankrupted an earlier company he was leading. The poor choices he made while strung out cost him everything and tanked the business.

He is now two years into his sobriety and is back leading a thriving corporation. However, he avoids conversations about his past because he believes the knowledge of his addiction would be unsettling for investors, employees, and clients, and undermine his overall leadership in the company. So he guts it out alone, pretending this part of his story never existed. But the problem is that it *did* exist, and he battles with that conflict every day. He isn't able to embrace his whole story and truly give himself a second chance. To fully understand redemption, we need to learn from our past failures.

After a few moments together, we reminded this tormented CEO what the great ninja warrior Warren Buffett once declared: "Every saint has a past, and every sinner has a future."

届 GIVE, RECEIVE, AND BE THE SECOND CHANCE

We live in a culture that is intoxicated with success. We love celebrity, stardom, and heroes. Stadiums are filled with adoring fans, and paparazzi love to chase down beautiful actresses. We idolize those with the best job titles and crave being invited to the green room.

We want to do things differently. People of the Second Chance rally behind the flops and the prodigals. We want to stand behind those who bet it all ... and came up short. We champion lost causes.

It is the quest to discover the limits of our own love and then learning to throw away those limits.

People of the Second Chance revolve around these core ideas:

忍者武士暗殺者

1. People of the Second Chance receive second chances in own lives. When we have experienced personal, professional, or relational failure, we refuse to be defined by our mistakes. We learn, we grow, and we have the courage to move on.

2. People of the Second Chance are individuals who forgive those who have wronged us. In a culture that believes in revenge and payback, we rebel with grace. It's about redefining grace – boundless, with no quid-pro-quos. Expecting – and sometimes getting – nothing back in return. It takes courage, strength, and total commitment to live like this.

Imagine if we no longer needed justice or payback. Would that not revolutionize our lives in profound ways? What if we stopped trying to hurt the already hurting?

3. People of the Second Chance pour our lives in places where people need second chances. We advocate for the vulnerable and fight for equality for the poor, the prisoner, and the voiceless. It is an action to stand with the broken. We are on the lookout for those who lives are falling apart and we respond.

These three core values can be simply summed up by:

Give, Receive, and Be the Second Chance.

盟 ROCK BOTTOM IS A GREAT FOUNDATION

J. K. Rowling, author of the Harry Potter juggernaut, gave a commencement speech at Harvard in 2008. In recalling her days when she was a divorced, single mom, almost homeless, she shared a few thoughts on failure:

"Failure meant a stripping away of the inessential. I stopped pretending to myself that I was anything other than what I was, and began to direct all my energy into finishing the only work that mattered to me. Had I really succeeded at anything else, I might never have found the determination to succeed in the one arena I believed I truly belonged. I was set free, because my greatest fear had already been realized, and I was still alive, and I still had a daughter whom I adored, and I had an old typewriter and a big idea. And so rock bottom became the solid foundation on which I rebuilt my life."

Welcome to the People of the Second Chance.

ABOUT THE AUTHORS

Mike Foster is the Creative Principal at PlainJoe Studios. In 2002, Mike founded XXXchurch, and led the creative vision of this organization until 2006. He and his wife, Jennifer, have two children and they live in Southern California.

Jud Wilhite lives in the Las Vegas area with his family where he leads Central Christian Church. He is the author of several books, including *Eyes Wide Open: See and Live the Real You* and *Uncensored Grace: Stories of Hope from the Streets of Vegas*.

Email Mike and Jud at mikeandjud@deadlyviper.org.

The Deadly Viper
Killer Experience

BUILT FOR ORGANIZATIONAL STAFFS, TEAMS, & SMALL GROUPS

Take your team, staff, or small group through this engaging and memorable character building excercise. Now you can start the conversation on important topics like character, integrity, and helping each other make killer choices. Master Po promises to turn your ninety-pound weaklings into buffed out warriors who are ready to slay the Character Assassins.

Here's what you get:
- 1 Deadly Viper Bundle of Books
- 1 Deadly Viper DVD
- Deadly Viper Group Conversation Starters
- Master Po's Leaders Guide
- Deadly Viper Fortune Cookies
- 1 Autographed copy of *Deadly Viper Character Assassins*

ORDER TODAY AT DEADLYVIPER.ORG

A portion of the profits from this book will go to the Shelter of Kuraburi, a social justice program serving single mothers living with AIDS in Thailand.

ethur

do good.

launching thought provoking and

creative initiatives to address

major cultural issues

www.ethur.org

节 ACKNOWLEDGMENTS

We owe a lot to these fine people and we are so truly thankful to:

Jennifer and Lori, for allowing us to marry way up!

Jackson, Taylor, Emma, and Ethan. You are why we do what we do.

Bill and Jean Foster and Carlos and Mary Wilhite. You have shown these two boys how to live with character.

Bill Townsend for "throwing fuel on the fire" and being an inspiring model of the principles in this book.

Marcus Buckingham, Duane Chapman, Craig Groeschel, Tony Hale, Joe Ritchie, Dan Cooper, Catherine Rohr, and Rabbi David Wolpe for sharing their wisdom and insights for *Deadly Viper*.

Peter McGowan for being a true friend and fellow warrior. Great to be on the journey with you.

Our buddies in the Dead Pastors Society who set the pace for all of us on transparency, leadership, and bravery.

We are in awe of our new friend Wess Stafford from Compassion International. It was an honor to eat hamster with you in Ecuador.

Brad Lomenick and Gabe Lyons for your support and belief in this project.

The Ethur staff and team: David Wever, Bruce Erickson, Tracy Carpenter, Elisa Carrasco, Kyle Koehler, Julie McDougall, Peter McGowan, Chris Ferebee, Blake Ryan, William Foster, and Brett Kerekffy.

The Central team for living these principles out every day.

The brilliant team at PlainJoe Studios. Especially to Ed McGowan and Suzanne Beaudoin for your incredible contribution to the layout and design. Johnny Davis for the sweet drawings, caricatures, and comic parables. Julie McDougall for the huge task of project management and to Sarah Dagley for project managing Mike. Christina Moseley for editing and Kai Husen for all your help through this process.

A huge thanks to the incredible team at Zondervan for their belief in and support of this project.

节 **ACKNOWLEDGMENTS (cont.)**

Thanks to Steve Paterson, Josh Webb, Tianna Buckwalter, Ron Duran, and Drew Ward for your beautiful design contributions. Your work was an amazing addition to the book.

Steve Wamberg and Jeff Brazil for reading through drafts of the book and providing excellent editorial insight.

Eric Cotter for the incredible photos. Calen Plouffe for your ninja skills. And to Kristen Foster and Sensei John Lipari from All American Karate for letting us play with swords and nunchucks for a day.

节 ENDNOTES

1 Jim Collins, "Is the Economy Just Built to Flip?" *Fast Company* (October 2002), 88.

2 Henry Cloud, *Integrity: The Courage to Meet the Demands of Reality* (New York: Harper Collins, 2007), 116-117.

3 Clive Thompson, "The See-Through CEO" *Wired*, Issue 15.04 (March 2007) (www.wired.com/wired/archive/15.04/wired40_ceo.html).

4 Cloud, *Integrity*, Ibid., 116.

5 Keith H. Hamonds, "Balance is Bunk," *Fast Company* (October 2004), 68 (www.fastcompany.com/magazine/87/balance-1.html).

6 Warren Buffett, as quoted at www.getrichslowly.org/blog/2006/12/19/the-billionaire-next-door-the-wisdom-of-warren-buffett/.

7 Joe Dominquez and Vicki Robin, *Your Money or Your Life: Transforming Your Relationship with Money and Achieving Financial Independence* (New York: Penguin, 1992).

8 D. G. Myers, "The Funds, Friends and Faith of Happy People," *American Psychologist* (Issue 55,2000), 56-67.

9 Pim Van Lommel, as quoted in Tijn Touber, "Life Goes On," *Ode* Vol. 3, Issue 10 (December, 2005).

10 Van Lommel, "Life Goes On," Ibid.

11 Jane Ann Morrison, "Judge Just Doesn't See Failure to Treat People with Dignity, Respect" *Las Vegas Review-Journal* (May 28, 2007) (www.lvrj.com/news/7714647.html).

12 Morrison, "Judge Just Doesn't See," Ibid.

Share Your Thoughts

With the Author: Your comments will be forwarded to the author when you send them to *zauthor@zondervan.com*.

With Zondervan: Submit your review of this book by writing to *zreview@zondervan.com*.

Free Online Resources at
www.zondervan.com

Zondervan AuthorTracker: Be notified whenever your favorite authors publish new books, go on tour, or post an update about what's happening in their lives.

Daily Bible Verses and Devotions: Enrich your life with daily Bible verses or devotions that help you start every morning focused on God.

Free Email Publications: Sign up for newsletters on fiction, Christian living, church ministry, parenting, and more.

Zondervan Bible Search: Find and compare Bible passages in a variety of translations at www.zondervanbiblesearch.com.

Other Benefits: Register yourself to receive online benefits like coupons and special offers, or to participate in research.